CW01052244

BUYING YOUR HOME WITH OTHER PEOPLE

Dave Treanor

The author and publishers would like to thank the
Abbey National Building Society
for the generous contribution which enabled us
to print and publish this guide.

Shelter & National Federation of Housing Associations

BUYING YOUR HOME
WITH OTHER PEOPLE

Dave Treanor

Published in December 1987 by Shelter and the National
Federation of Housing Associations
88 Old Street, London EC1V 9HU
© Shelter & National Federation of Housing Associations

Typesetting: Lifespan Printing Collective, Barnsley
Paste-up: Blackrose Press (TU), London EC1
Printed and bound in Great Britain by A. Wheaton & Co. Ltd.,
Exeter
Trade distribution: Turnaround 01-609 7836

Cover illustration: Judy Stevens
Cover design: Spencers Ltd. (TU), London EC1

Illustrations throughout by Judy Stevens

British Library Cataloguing in Publication Data
Treanor, Dave
    Buying your home with other people
    1. House buying — England
    I. Treanor, Dave
    643.12′0942 HD1379

ISBN 0-901242-79-9

Dedicated to

David Bristow

whose help and advice was invaluable to the development
of the co-operative housing movement.

Acknowledgements

This book developed from a project initially funded by the Joseph Rowntree Memorial Trust. The early research was carried out by Jill Gundry and Euan Ramsay at the National Federation of Housing Associations (NFHA), who also produced an early draft and laid down the basic specification for the book.

Steve Ross and Euan Ramsay of the NFHA provided regular guidance through the research and writing of the book which was funded by the NFHA. Tony Trott of the Empty Property Unit at Shelter and other members of the National Federation of Housing Co-operatives' Mortgage Finance Group provided invaluable information and constructive criticism. Simon Erskine and Richard Robertson offered a great deal of useful experience arising from many years' work as accountants to mortgage-funded housing co-ops and other joint ownership ventures.

James Sinclair Taylor, of Sinclair Taylor and Martin, developed the trust deed on which the chapter on trusts is based, and gave his time generously in advice based on many years' experience as a solicitor working with groups of people wanting to buy their housing together. Sinclair Taylor and Martin kindly gave permission for their trust deed to be reproduced in Appendix A. Other legal advice came from David Marcus of Franks Charlesley and Company.

Mike McQueen of the Nationwide, Tim Canniffe and Stephen Smith of the Abbey National, and Ray Bell of the Halifax all helped to explain the ways in which building societies would view the joint ownership schemes covered by the book.

Sally Thomas and John Gatward of the Housing Corporation gave advice on housing co-operatives and Tony Shephard advised on co-ownerships.

Several people helped by reading the early drafts and commenting from their own experience of living in joint-ownership schemes of one sort or another. Jonathan Shopley made some particularly useful suggestions for ways of introducing the reader more gently to some of the more complex issues.

Contents

CHAPTER 1

Introduction

This Book Looks At Some......

WAYS PEOPLE CAN SHARE THE OWNERSHIP OF THEIR HOUSING

The scope of this book

This book looks at the different ways people can share the ownership of their housing. They might be a small group of two or three friends who cannot afford to buy the sort of property they want as individuals. They might be part of a larger scheme of a dozen or more people, with a mixture of self-contained and shared facilities. Or they might be a group of tenants wishing to take control of their own housing, perhaps in order to improve their street or neighbourhood and overcome common problems ranging from loneliness to vandalism.

In recent years a number of ways of sharing the ownership of housing have been developed. People's reasons for wanting to co-own vary enormously, and this book tries to avoid making any assumptions about what yours might be. It concentrates on practicalities, such as how to raise a mortgage, and whether or not you qualify for Housing Benefit as a tenant would, or for the grants and subsidies available to home owners.

The advice is based on the experience of a range of successful schemes and of a number of accountants and solicitors who have worked with joint ownerships. The advice on raising finance has been discussed with those building societies that have taken the lead in lending on joint ownerships of one type or another, notably the Abbey National, Nationwide, and Halifax building societies.

There is a focus on the smaller schemes suitable for anything up to fifty households, set up with loans from banks or building societies, taking advantage of any grants and subsidies available. Although some of the options could be developed on a larger scale, the implications of doing so and other possibilities that might be considered are not covered.

Factors affecting your choice

The alternatives
Variations on the four main forms of joint ownership are described. These are:
- *Trusts*, through which a group of friends can share ownership of a house;
- *Leasehold*, whereby you share the freehold but each

hold your own lease on a self-contained unit, with
scope for some shared facilities;

- *Co-ownerships*, in which larger numbers of people
  can share ownership of either self-contained units,
  shared housing, or some combination of the two,
  while retaining most of the advantages of being
  owner occupiers;
- *Housing co-operatives*, in which the members are
  essentially tenants sharing the responsibilities of
  the landlord. Although they collectively own the
  property they have no personal stake in its value.

There are good and bad things that can be said about
each approach, and it would be best to read through
this guide and think about them all before deciding
which is the right one for you. There are a number of
factors that might influence your choice:

The size of your group
Complexity can rise rapidly with numbers. Once a
group gets above half a dozen or so the emphasis
needs to shift from defining each person's rights and
responsibilities to creating a democratic framework
within which to share management responsibility. A
small group is more dependent on individual re-
lationships to hold it together, whereas a larger one
needs to rise above them, so that individuals can
come and go without too much disruption to everyone else.

The way larger groups usually deal with this is to
register a separate legal body to own the property,
such as a co-ownership society or a housing co-operative. This involves having your accounts audited
each year, and making an annual report to the Registrar of Friendly Societies, who also has to approve
your rules. Individuals join or leave, but the corporate body lives on until you collectively decide to
dissolve it. There should be at least seven people to
form one of these.

Co-ownerships and housing co-operatives are described in chapters 6, 7 and 8.

In small groups of up to half a dozen it is usually simplest to vest ownership in the individuals, and reach agreements to cover managing the property they share and what happens if one or other of them wants to leave. A trust is most likely to suit their needs. Or, if you intend to live in relatively self-contained flats, you might jointly own the freehold, with each household holding a long lease on its own unit.

These are purely private arrangements between yourselves which, with good legal advice, can be tailored to your specific requirements. Trusts and leasehold arrangements are described in chapters 4 and 5.

Shared facilities
The second factor is the extent to which you want shared facilities. Most people going in for joint ownership do so for a combination of reasons, amongst which is usually some desire to share with their neighbours

You may want your own self-contained flat, and to limit any sharing to the use of the garden and the right to some say in who your neighbours are. Rural groups often share the grounds and some workshops in the outbuildings.

Providing a front door with its own separate access to the outside is usually the hardest part of converting urban houses into self-contained units. Also you may prefer to have easy access to your friends living in other parts of the house. It is possible to have semi-self-contained units within a larger house, creating separate households with some shared facilities, such as a laundry, and even some common living rooms.

Some go further and cook and eat their main evening meal together, with facilities in their members' own units for cooking small meals.

At the other extreme are those living together as one household, in which everything except their own bedroom is shared.

Although lenders are becoming much more flexible these days, they still feel safer lending to separate households living in self-contained units. Raising a mortgage is likely to be more complicated for you the more you intend to share. Estate agents may be reluctant to show you their easier to sell properties – the sort building societies like – for fear of complications with which they have little previous experience.

If dividing the property into self-contained units fits in with what you want to do, it will generally be easier to raise the money. Against that, the conversions might add to the costs of a scheme. You can often fit more people comfortably into a shared house than the same building divided into flats.

If you are planning to have self-contained units, the leasehold arrangements in chapter 5 or the leasehold co-ownership described in chapter 6 are generally the best options. Or you might consider a shared ownership scheme along the lines suggested in chapter 8.

Those intending to share facilities are more likely to prefer to set up a trust like the one described in chapter 4; or if they are a larger group they would be better off as a co-ownership society or housing co-operative. These are described in chapters 6 and 7.

Bureaucracy
It takes longer and costs more to set up a co-op or co-ownership, because your rules have to be approved by the Registrar of Friendly Societies. In the relevant chapters you will also discover about seeking approval from the Department of the Environment, and registering with the Housing Corporation, in order to qualify for benefits automatically available to owner

occupiers. All of this involves a certain amount of bureaucratic interference.

From this point of view a trust or leasehold arrangement is much simpler. You need go no further than your solicitor who can work it all out for you on the spot, and will probably not charge more than £150 to £250 for a trust, or a similar amount for each lease agreement.

But there are dangers in trust arrangements just because they are so flexible. Your lawyer may not be sufficiently familiar with their use in joint ownership of housing to advise on all the possible pitfalls. There is no 'outside body' watching over the trustees to ensure that everything is conducted fairly in the best interests of everyone concerned. There are no national organisations to represent the common interests of people in trusts, and point out any adverse changes in law or practice that are being contemplated. To a much larger extent than with other options, a trust is on its own.

Owner or tenant?

Most of this book is about ways in which a group of people can share the benefit of being joint owner occupiers, including the right to sell their share of the property for whatever it is worth when then want to move on.

But there are those who want to share their housing without necessarily having a stake in the value of the property. It is much easier for people to come and go if there is no need to buy and sell their share of the property. The best way of doing this is to form a housing co-operative.

The money paid to people when they leave as their share of the increased value of the house does not magically appear out of the bricks and mortar as one of the mysterious properties of inflation: it is usually paid by somebody new moving in to replace them.

The trouble is that after a few years of rising house prices, the amount of money involved can be rather large. There may not be very many people with enough savings to put in as a cash deposit.

Joint home ownership is only viable in the longer term if new people buying into it can raise a mortgage loan with which to pay for their share of the property. How easy this may be is discussed for each of the schemes described in this book.

Where householders own a long lease on a self-contained unit it is generally simple enough: the mortgage can be secured against the value of the lease itself. Where people are sharing a house, the whole property has to be remortgaged. Some building societies are reluctant to lend for joint ownership of shared housing because of this implied liability to remortgage in order to repay someone leaving. Fortunately there are many building societies, and not all of them take this view.

The fact that those buying in later pay more than those who were there from the beginning has other implications: after a few years of high inflation the difference in what it costs the newcomers to live in the same place can be very considerable. If you live in self-contained flats it is relatively easy to distance yourself from this sort of inequality, but if you live together it can become a serious problem.

It is for this reason that those who choose to share their housing often prefer to form a housing co-operative. Not only does it reduce problems of inequality within the group, but it keeps the cost of housing down for everyone concerned. The converse is also true: those who want a stake in the value of their housing usually end up in relatively self-contained units.

On the other hand, people who have lived for a number of years in housing co-operatives that they may have set up themselves can find it hard to move on. As inflation reduces the real cost of loan re-payments, it will have become relatively cheap to live in their shared house. People who join later benefit from the low rents that may have been relatively expensive at first for the original group. And yet when one of those original people wants to leave they find they have to start all over again, either paying a full market rent to stay somewhere else, or somehow finding the money for a deposit and the full mortgage payments to buy their own home.

The chapter on co-ownership looks at other ways of tackling some of the problems of inequality arising from inflation in the price of property. These issues are discussed as they arise in describing co-owner-ship and co-operatives in chapters 6 and 7.

How to use this book

There is a growing demand from those wishing to share the ownership of their housing in one form or another, but it is a relatively new field. This book brings together some of the more successful approaches, but it cannot draw up a simple list of 'the best buys'. As you read on you will find a maze of variations on the main themes.

This first chapter introduces the four basic alterna-tives: trusts, leaseholds, co-ownership societies and co-operatives. It indicates some of the factors that might affect your choice, such as the size of your group, and the extent to which you want to live collectively or separately. It highlights the choice between being joint owners or sharing as tenants within a collectively owned housing scheme.

The idea is to provide a starting point for the explo-ration of your own choices. The 'Choice Chart' on page 18 is an over-simplification, and is intended only as a guide that might save you wading through chap-ters on irrelevant options before reaching the ones most suitable to your own requirements.

It is unlikely that solicitors would have a ready-made package to suit your requirements. You cannot assume they will be familiar with all the options you should be considering. It is not their job to tell you what would be the best for you, for which they would need experience of a number of joint ownership schemes. Their job is to tell you how to get what you want, which means you must be clear amongst yourselves about what you are trying to achieve.

This book sets out to describe each option and what it entails, and to look at the factors that should affect your choice. It is important that each individual member of the group understands the implications. Do they want an individual stake in the value of the house so that they can sell their share when they leave? What are their reasons for sharing, and just how much self-containment would they prefer?

At some point one or other of you will want to leave. Each person should think about it from their own point of view. Suppose they themselves wanted to leave: what would they expect? Could they find someone else they would want to share with if any of the others left? These are all essential subjects for discussion amongst the group. This book aims to provide information that will enable each of you to participate fully in the process.

Before signing anything, the whole group should have the opportunity to discuss what they are doing with their professional advisers. In a large group it is a good idea to set up a meeting at which your solicitor, and perhaps your accountant, can explain what is being proposed and answer any questions you may have. In a smaller group you should all meet your solicitor to discuss the options and implications of the agreements you are making before you sign anything.

Choice chart: a simple guide to the alternatives

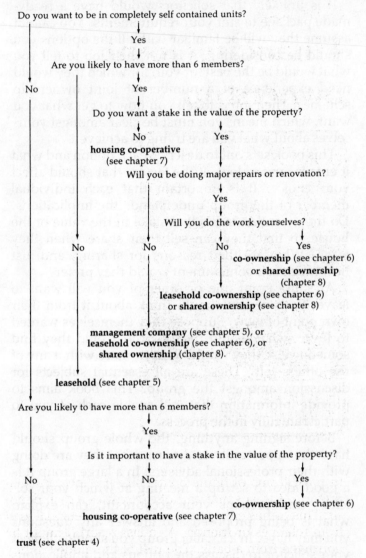

Do you want to be in completely self contained units?
↓
Yes
↓
Are you likely to have more than 6 members?

No   Yes
↓
Do you want a stake in the value of the property?

No   Yes
housing co-operative
(see chapter 7)
Will you be doing major repairs or renovation?
↓
Yes
↓
Will you do the work yourselves?

No   No   No   Yes
co-ownership (see chapter 6)
or **shared ownership**
(chapter 8)
leasehold co-ownership (see chapter 6)
or **shared ownership** (see chapter 8)
management company (see chapter 5), or
leasehold co-ownership (see chapter 6), or
shared ownership (chapter 8).

leasehold (see chapter 5)

Are you likely to have more than 6 members?
↓
Yes
↓
Is it important to have a stake in the value of the property?

No   No   Yes
co-ownership (see chapter 6)
housing co-operative (see chapter 7)

trust (see chapter 4)

There are a number of other factors to take into account in working out the
best form of joint ownership for your group. To appreciate the options fully you
will have to read about them all. This diagram is offered as a guide to provide you
with a starting point from which to consider the alternatives.

CHAPTER 2

Financing joint ownership

In most forms of home ownership it is necessary to provide at least some part of the cost as a cash deposit. This comes either from savings or a personal loan from relatives or friends. As a last resort it might be borrowed from a bank. The rest of the money to buy the property comes from a combination of grants and a mortgage loan.

The first part of this chapter looks at mortgage

loans. The second part briefly describes the grants that may be available to finance improvements or repair of the property. At the end is a checklist of the sorts of costs and charges that go to make up the total development cost of the property.

Most technical terms are defined in the glossary (page 167). If you do not understand a piece of jargon, look it up there.

Mortgage loans

The usual way of borrowing money to buy a house is through a mortgage loan. The loan is 'secured' against the value of the property. If you should fail to pay up, the lender can sell the property and take what is owed to them from the proceeds before passing the rest of the money back to the borrower.

When you take out a mortgage loan, the lender registers their 'interest' in the property on the title deeds at the Land Registry.

Most mortgage loans are made by building societies or banks, although there is no reason why an individual should not lend under a mortgage arrangement.

Mortgage tax relief and MIRAS

Home owners are entitled to tax relief on the interest element of their mortgage payments on loans of up to £30,000 for the purchase or improvement of their main residence (1987 values). At the moment this is cumulative for joint owners unless they are married, so that for example, four joint owners would be eligible for tax relief on a £120,000 mortgage. There are suggestions that the rules will soon be changed, limiting tax relief to £30,000 per dwelling.

House prices are affected by the amount people can afford to pay. There is an argument that because tax relief increases the mortgage people can afford, it merely puts up the price of housing. It benefits home owners at the expense of the private rented sector. There is some political debate on a proposal to abolish it altogether, particularly because it is a subsidy that provides the greatest benefit to the better off.

Tax relief can be obtained through the Pay As You Earn (PAYE) tax coding system, or through a refund at the end of the tax year. But the most common way of obtaining tax relief is through MIRAS. Under the Mortgage Interest Relief at Source (MIRAS) scheme, an approved lender reduces the interest charged to you by the equivalent of tax relief at the basic rate of tax. The lender then claims the tax relief from the Inland Revenue. All the high street banks and building societies are approved under the scheme, so that in practice almost all mortgages, except those arranged through private individuals, fall within it. Even if you are on a low income and pay no tax, you still get the benefit of the same subsidy.

How large a mortgage loan can you borrow?

The size of the loan depends on two things: the security of the loan, and your ability to afford the repayments.

As far as security is concerned, the lender will want to be sure that if they have to sell the property to get their money back it will fetch enough to cover the loan. On older properties they do not usually lend more than 85% of their valuation. This valuation may be less than you are paying for the property. They may wish to play even safer with the sort of large old property you are likely to be buying, and you could find they lend only 70% of the money you need, or less. If you need to borrow more than that the lender may require a 'one-off' insurance payment, sometimes referred to as a 'mortgage guarantee', to protect them against the value of the property being insufficient to cover the loan. The premium could cost 2% to 2½% of the extra loan borrowed above their limit. Even so you will rarely be able to borrow 100% of the valuation except on new housing. The cost of this insurance is usually added onto the loan and paid for through the mortgage payments.

They will also be concerned about your ability to make the repayments. They will favour anyone with a good mortgage record. This is likely to concern them less if you are borrowing a relatively small proportion of the total valuation. Naturally enough they prefer an easy to sell property in a popular district, whereas you may well want to buy a less conventional type of building in a cheap neighbourhood. Do be prepared to negotiate. Put your best suit on and sell yourself. Above all, avoid worrying them with irrelevant detail on the arrangements you are making between yourselves. A detailed and professional application is more likely to succeed than a vague request for a loan.

A lender will make their own assessment of how much you can afford to borrow relative to your income. As a rough rule of thumb they might lend an individual borrower two and a half to three times their gross annual income. In practice, branch managers are not as rigid as that, and will take account of a variety of other circumstances. With two owners they sometimes lend up to three times the higher income plus the full amount of the lower. There is no simple guide to the amount they will lend joint owners, although one large building society has said they would lend up to three times the income of the higher earners, plus the full income of the rest.

Different types of mortgage

Conventional annuity mortgages may start off very

expensive, but they get cheaper in real terms as time passes. This is because the repayments stay more or less the same while inflation reduces the real value of money. The only thing that affects the cost of the mortgage to you is a change in the rate of interest being charged.

At the same time house prices tend to rise, so that someone buying today might be paying twice as much as their next-door neighbour who bought an almost identical house five years ago. People have come to expect to sell their house after a few years for considerably more than they originally paid. The cash gain is usually used as a deposit on a better house.

First-time buyers are at a double disadvantage: they do not have the capital gain from the sale of a previous home, and because they tend to be younger their incomes are generally lower. Several schemes have been devised to help first-time buyers. They all aim to reduce the repayments in the first years of a mortgage, at the cost of higher payments later. In effect this enables people on lower incomes to raise a larger loan than would otherwise have been possible on their income.

These 'low-start' loans will only be appropriate in certain circumstances, and will be much harder to obtain than conventional mortgages. If they were more widely available they would be self-defeating, because by raising the limits on what people could afford to borrow they would push up the price of housing. Such loans are more suited to housing co-operatives or co-ownerships, than to trusts or lease-hold arrangements.

Index-linking
In return for low initial repayments, the borrower of an index-linked mortgage agrees to increase their payments by the rate of inflation each year. The cost

of their mortgage repayments will rise with inflation, so that in real 'value of money' terms the cost of buying the house is spread more evenly over the term of the mortgage.

The repayments consist of a relatively low fixed-interest payment (currently 4½% before any tax relief), and repayment of the capital on the outstanding loan. The amount outstanding on your loan is also increased each year by the rate of inflation.

The result is that initial repayments on an index-linked mortgage are roughly half those on a conventional one, so that for the same income you can borrow twice as much money.

But there are a number of disadvantages:

- You may have to pay a heavy penalty for early redemption of an index-linked mortgage. This would amount to a surcharge for selling the house in the early years of the mortgage.
- Even though you might sell the house for more than you paid for it after a few years, you will make a relatively small capital gain to use as a deposit on a better one. This is because the amount you owe is increased each year in line with inflation.
- Building societies are reluctant to lend more than 85% of the valuation because of the risk that the value of your particular house might not rise sufficiently to keep pace with inflation. Mortgage guarantees from insurance companies that might encourage the lender to advance nearer 100% of the valuation will be more expensive for the same reasons.
- The tax relief subsidy on the interest is relatively small, being payable on the interest but not on the money added each year to the outstanding loan. You end up with less than half the subsidy normally paid on a conventional mortgage.
- A relatively large proportion of the repayments are

of capital and would not be covered by the DHSS for an owner who was unemployed or on supplementary benefit.

Index-linked mortgages are most likely to be relevant where the loan is raised by a body set up to own the property, such as a housing co-operative or co-ownership scheme. So long as individuals can come and go without the need to remortgage the property, the surcharge on early repayment of the mortgage is avoided. The members can then benefit from lower initial mortgage repayments at the expense of the profit available from the sale of their share of the property.

Index-linked loans are sometimes combined with a conventional annuity mortgage so that only part of the loan is index-linked.

The Halifax and the Nationwide building societies have taken the lead in pioneering index-linked mortgages. They have to match their lending to index-linked funds they themselves borrow. As a result, such mortgages are not available to home owners generally and are unlikely to be appropriate on small schemes.

Deferred interest

Repayments on a deferred-interest mortgage start off low, but the borrower agrees to increase them by a fixed rate each year. The difference between this and the amount that would have been paid under a conventional mortgage is added each year to the outstanding loan.

As with index-linking, the amount you owe increases in the early years of the mortgage. As a result you suffer from some of the same disadvantages, although there is no penalty if you sell up in the early years:

• A large part of any increase in value of the property will go towards repaying the deferred payments that were added to the outstanding loan.

- Because your debt rises, the lender will be anxious to ensure that the amount you owe will always be adequately covered by the rising value of the property.
- Mortgage guarantees from an insurance company that might encourage the building societies to lend a larger part of the cost of buying the house will be correspondingly harder to obtain and more expensive.
- You qualify for tax relief on the interest paid in each year, but not on the deferred-interest payments that are added to the outstanding loan. The interest paid on these additions to the outstanding loan is unlikely to be subsidised.
- Tax relief may have to be claimed either through the PAYE tax coding system or as a refund from the Inland Revenue, as it is not generally available under the MIRAS scheme. (In that case those not paying tax could lose the benefit: check this with the lender and your local Inland Revenue office.)

One advantage over an index-linked loan is that in the first half of the life of the loan the payments are mostly of interest, on which a house owner can get help from the DHSS if they are unemployed or on supplementary benefit.

Against this, the initial repayments on deferred-interest loans are likely to be higher than those on index-linked loans.

Deferred-interest loans are not generally available, but they are more widely available from building societies than index-linked loans. Banks are unlikely to offer them.

Other forms of low-start loans

Some building societies operate a form of low-start mortgage under which the borrower pays a deposit when they buy the house, which is used to subsidise the payments in the first three or four years, so that they are able to borrow a larger amount than would otherwise have been justifiable on their income. The assumption is that their income will rise each year in real terms, enabling them to meet the rising re-payments in the first years of the mortgage.

These loans are usually only available on the type of property on which a building society might be prepared to lend close to 100% of the cost of purchase.

There is no loss of tax relief, and there are no particular problems over DHSS payments if the borrower becomes unemployed or goes onto supplementary benefit. Once the period of reduced payments is passed, it becomes no different from a conventional mortgage.

This form of low-start mortgage is a clever way of using the money a buyer pays in cash for their house for two things at once: it is used to bridge the difference between the purchase price and the amount the building society would be prepared to lend against the value of the property, and it is used to reduce the initial repayments.

This type of loan is suitable for purchases in which the individual takes out a mortgage loan in their own name, such as with conventional home ownership; but it could also apply to the leasehold arrangements in chapter 5, or the leasehold co-ownership schemes in chapter 6.

The initial mortgage payments, however, are only reduced for the first three or four years, and will be higher than on an index-linked or deferred-interest mortgage. Low-start mortgages are not available from all building societies, and will only be available under limited circumstances in schemes aimed at making a form of home ownership available to those who could not otherwise afford it.

Equity mortgages

Under new legislation, building societies will be able to offer an 'equity mortgage'. The borrower owns the house, but the lender takes a proportion of the equity growth, in exchange for a lower interest rate. In other words, part of the increase in value of the property goes to the lender in exchange for lower mortgage repayments. There may be a requirement for the borrower to buy the remaining equity from the lender within a certain period.

The lender will want to be confident that the house will appreciate in value, and not deteriorate significantly during the term of the loan. Consequently they will be more than usually concerned about the condition of the building, and are likely to prefer recently renovated or new property.

Most of the initial mortgage payments are of interest. Unlike most other types of mortgage designed to reduce the cost of initial payments, tax relief is available on the whole of the interest, in exactly the same way as with a conventional mortgage.

At present this is all theoretical, since no building society is offering equity mortgages suitable for joint ownership. Until they do we can only surmise on the likely terms. The Woolwich Building Society is offering a form of equity mortgage to people buying houses built by one of their subsidiaries.

The shared ownership schemes operate on a similar principle. In these a housing association, or sometimes a local authority, provides housing in which the tenant can buy part of the equity. Shared ownership could be a step towards home ownership for those who could not otherwise afford it. Ways in which it might be adapted for use by those wishing to own property jointly are discussed in chapter 8.

Where to go for a mortgage

Building societies were set up to provide loans to people wanting to buy their own homes. For several years now banks have also been actively lending on mortgages.

Your initial approach might be through the local branch office, but for larger schemes you should approach the regional manager or the head office. The local branch should be able to tell you who to contact.

The larger national building societies, particularly the Halifax, Abbey National and the Nationwide, have more experience of lending on joint ownership, and have been consulted in writing this book. The smaller local societies may also be able to help, and might consider your case on its own merits.

Building societies sometimes claim to give preference to people who have had substantial savings invested with them, particularly when funds are in short supply.

A reputable mortgage broker could help you find the right lender or a more suitable type of mortgage if your initial approaches to the building societies or banks do not succeed. But you may have to ask around to find one who understands what you are trying to do.

Home improvement and other grants

There are four types of grant available through local authorities. Of these, only one, the Intermediate Grant, is mandatory. The others are discretionary, and depend on the availability of resources within the relevant local authority budget, which in itself is controlled by the government. Further details should be available from the local authority. All figures quoted in this section are based on 1986 levels unless otherwise stated.

Local authority grants are available to owner occupiers and on rented property, so that almost all joint ownership schemes should be eligible. The grants are not available to anyone renovating property for sale.

Intermediate Grants

The grant applies to a dwelling built or converted before 1961 that has been without a bath or some other 'standard amenity' for over a year. These amenities include a kitchen sink, indoor toilet, and plumbing hot and cold water to a bath or any other essential facility.

There is a table of maximum expenses allowable for each amenity. If you spend more, the grant will be based on the allowable amount, 75% of which qualifies for a grant (this can be raised to 90% in cases of hardship).

At the same time a grant may be made to put the dwelling into 'reasonable repair'. The maximum is a little over £4000 in London and £3000 elsewhere.

Special Grants

These grants are discretionary, and apply only to hostels and other dwellings in multiple occupation. They may be available to cover the provision or improvement of standard amenities and means of escape from fire.

If a local authority serves a notice requiring the works to be done, the grant becomes mandatory.

In 1986 the maximum grant for a fire escape was £8000 (£10,000 in London), and for other repairs was £3000 (£4200 in London).

Improvement Grants

This local authority grant is intended to bring a home up to a reasonable standard or to convert one house into two or more dwelling units. The local authority will require assurances that the conversion will have at least a 30 year life, that repairs will be done to a reasonable standard, that the property will be damp-proofed and structurally stable, and that it will have all standard amenities.

The house must have been built before 1961 or be lacking standard amenities. In addition its rateable value must not exceed £225 (£400 in London), or £350 (£600 in London) in the case of a conversion into more than one unit.

The size of the grant depends on whether the property is in an area that has been declared a 'Housing Action Area' by the local authority. The grant is usually up to 50% of costs, but in a Housing Action Area can be anything up to 90% of the cost of improvement. However, the relevant Secretary of State for housing has the power to over-rule the declaration of a Housing Action Area by a local authority; these powers have already been used, for instance to prevent higher improvement grants being applied to co-ops formed by tenants on some peripheral estates in Glasgow.

Once again, there are limits on the level of expenditure on which grant is payable. The limits range from a maximum of £16,000 (a London, priority case, conversion) to a minimum of £6,600 (outside London, non-priority case, improvement). Additional levels are allowed for listed buildings.

Very few local authorities were providing significant amounts of Improvement Grant in 1986 due to restrictions on their capital budgets imposed by the government.

Repair Grants
These grants are also discretionary unless a 'repairs notice' is served by the local authority, in which case they become mandatory.

To qualify, the house must have been built before 1919, have a rateable value of less than £225 (£400 in London), and be in need of both substantial and structural repairs. These might include repairs to roof, chimneys, walls, doors, windows, foundations, and floors. Repair grants may also be available to replace lead pipes.

The grant is normally 75% of the eligible expense limit, which in 1984 was £6,600 in London and £4,400 elsewhere, with small extra amounts for listed buildings.

Insulation Grants

Local authorities can provide grants covering two-thirds of the cost of insulating roof spaces, tanks and pipework up to a limit of £69 per dwelling. In special cases, the grant can be for 90% of the cost up to a limit of £95. Special cases include households with a disabled person or old age pensioners in receipt of supplementary benefit or housing benefit.

Housing Association Grant

Housing associations and housing co-ops that are registered with the Housing Corporation can qualify for Housing Association Grant (HAG) either through the Housing Corporation itself or through a local authority. The grant usually covers the difference between the cost of providing the housing and the loan to be repaid with income from 'fair rents' charged on it. It is also used to fund major repairs, or in combination with mortgage funding to bring rents down to levels affordable by those in greatest housing need.

HAG is the main source of funding for housing associations, and it is beyond the scope of this book to explain it in any detail. The National Federation of Housing Associations can supply more information. Their book 'Development − a guide for small housing associations' explains the way HAG works.

Where to find out about these grants
Part of an architect's job is to advise their clients on what grants are available, and the most economic ways of achieving their requirements. For more general information you could try your local Citizen's Advice Bureau, or go straight to the housing department of your local authority.

Check list of costs and charges

In addition to the purchase price for the property, there will be a number of fees and charges to pay when a property is bought. These might include:

- Stamp duty at 1% of the purchase price over £30,000.
- Land Registry fees, in areas where registration is compulsory.
- Solicitors' fees for setting up your joint-ownership arrangements, and for administering the purchase and mortgage on the property. Large building societies usually use your solicitors to act for them in drawing up the mortgage agreement. Smaller societies may charge you for use of their own solicitors.
- Surveyors' fees – you will have to pay the lender's survey fee, and would be well advised to pay for a report to satisfy your own concerns about the condition of the property.
- Planning permission is necessary wherever there is a change of use or of external design, for which there is a charge ranging upwards from £40.
- Architects' fees where conversion works are required.
- Development agents' fees where you use a professional body to manage the purchase and renovation or building of the property.

- Insurance of the property. The lender will insist that this is sufficient to cover any mortgage loan; it is up to you to ensure that it is sufficient to cover the full replacement value of the buildings. It is normally paid annually.
- Registration fees where you are forming a company, housing association, or housing co-operative.
- Mortgage guarantee or insurance where you wish to borrow a higher proportion of the value of the property than the lender is prepared to advance on the security of the property alone.

These expenses should be included in the total development costs of the property and taken into account in assessing the amount of money you need to raise. Consult your solicitor to check that you have a complete list of the charges that will apply to you.

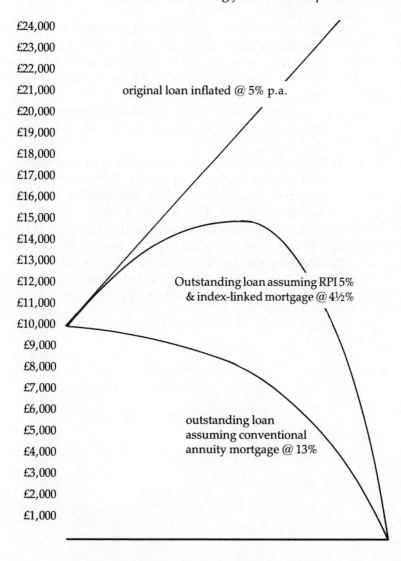

Graph showing how the amount owed on a £10,000 index-linked mortgage rises with inflation, but not as fast as the real inflated value of the original loan.

CHAPTER 3

Tenancies

OWNERS EXPECT FINANCIAL GAIN –
BUT A TENANT LEAVES WITH NOTHING.

What is a tenancy?

A tenant is someone who occupies a dwelling in exchange for rent. Post-war governments introduced all sorts of rules to try and prevent landlords exploiting the shortage of housing by taking advantage of the vulnerability of tenants.

Private landlords are governed by the Rent Acts.

Most of their tenants are 'protected tenants' under the 1977 Rent Act. This prevents the landlord evicting them except where a court accepts that they have broken their tenancy agreement, or on certain other specific grounds.

Housing association and local authority tenancies are governed by the Housing Acts. Most of their tenants are 'secure tenants' under the 1980 Housing Act (now consolidated into the 1985 Housing Act). This means that they cannot be evicted except on specific grounds laid down by law, such as for persistent rent arrears.

The government has announced proposals for new legislation that will exempt most new tenancies from rent control.

People sharing a house as joint owners under most of the schemes described in this book would not be regarded as tenants. The only exception applies to the members of a housing co-operative. Nevertheless, there may be circumstances in which you want to have others living with you who are not owners, and have no stake in the value of the property.

There are problems that can arise from having two classes of people sharing a house. Owners expect some financial gain from rising house prices, whereas a tenant leaves with nothing. If the owners should decide to sell up, the tenants could find themselves without a home. Improvements to the property may make everyone more comfortable. But any increase in the value of the property arising as a result of tenants' work or paid for out of their rents belongs exclusively to those who own the property. These differences can lead to widely divergent attitudes, which may only surface at times of conflict, or when someone wants to leave.

The legal position
A bank or building society is unlikely to make a mortgage loan unless they can be sure of obtaining vacant possession of the property should you breach the terms of your mortgage agreement, particularly if you fail to keep up the mortgage payments. An occupied house is worth much less than a vacant one, and they will want to be sure that your house is worth at least as much as the money they have loaned you.

Anyone who has a stake in the value of the property is treated as an owner, and not as a tenant. The building society can get them out by going to a court and obtaining a possession order on the house. This means that no one participating in a joint-ownership scheme who has the right to a share in the value of the property will be protected as a tenant under the Rent Acts.

Landlord and tenant legislation is quite complex, and likely to be changed in a new housing bill shortly to be introduced in Parliament. A Citizen's Advice Bureau or local Community Law Centre should be able to answer specific questions about tenants' rights. It would be beyond the scope of this book to define what constitutes a protected or secure tenancy. The following sections explain the most relevant principles as they apply at present.

Security of tenure under existing legislation
Most tenancies are secure. You may have heard about licences to occupy property, but following a recent House of Lords ruling, all licences are probably in fact tenancies, unless the person really is a lodger or genuinely does not have exclusive use of any space, even a bedroom.

There are three ways you can have people living with you without them getting substantial security:
- As a lodger, which means they can have their own room and pay a rent, but they must receive some

essential service, such as cleaning of their room, provision of meals or doing their laundry. This must be more than a token service or the courts will see it as a way of avoiding the creation of a secure tenancy and ignore it.

- A tenancy where there is genuine sharing of essential living space. Sharing bathroom and toilet is not enough. Sharing a kitchen or living room would be. To be certain you should have a clearly written occupancy agreement that stipulates the facilities they share. (The sample Occupancy Agreement in Appendix C could be used for this purpose, modified where the group is not a co-op.)

- As tenant of a property where the landlord's principle home is in the same house. This is probably the most likely category for joint-ownership arrangements (except where the landlord is a corporate body such as a co-op or company), but do check your particular circumstances with a lawyer before trusting that you are not creating a protected tenancy.

A lodger is not a tenant and can be asked to leave at reasonable notice. The other two approaches listed above create tenancies that are not secure or protected tenancies in terms of the Rent Acts.

Tenants are entitled to Housing Benefit where they are on a low income or unemployed, providing they do not have a share in the value of the property. A lodger can receive a 'lodgings allowance' from the DHSS including the cost of accommodation and essential services provided.

Effects of proposed legislation
Under the government's proposals all new tenancies will be either 'shorthold' or 'assured' tenancies:

Shorthold tenancies will be for a fixed period of at least 6 months. Tenants will have no right to renew the tenancy. Rents will be controlled at a market rent taking account of their limited security of tenure.

Assured tenancies will provide security of tenure on a basis similar to protected tenancies under existing legislation, but at a rent to be agreed between landlord and tenant.

Existing tenancies will be largely unaffected. But once a dwelling is vacated it will be let on the new basis. New tenancies will not be subject to fair rents.

Housing associations and co-ops will be governed by the same rules as private landlords. Remaining rent controls will be removed from resident landlords.

The lender's position
As far as a lender of a mortgage loan on the property is concerned, a tenancy you create is only secure if they acknowledge it. This is true even if they know about it. This means that if they take possession following some breach of the mortgage agreement, they can evict anyone whose tenancy they have not acknowledged.

This does not apply if the tenant was living in the house at the time the mortgage agreement was signed, in which case the lender could not evict them in repossessing the property. This is why lenders may require all those who have not signed the mortgage agreement to sign a form of consent to the mortgage. In this they simply acknowledge that any rights they may have, such as to live in the property, are subject to the superior rights of the lender under its mortgage.

Tenants of a housing co-operative cannot have their security limited in this way. In effect the lender is assumed to have acknowledged their tenancy since letting property is part of the essential purpose of the co-op. There are other ways of ensuring that tenancies created by a co-op are not secure tenancies.

These are discussed in the chapter on housing co-operatives.

If the property is tenanted the initial valuation will be much less than if it were vacant. A building society may be prepared to lend on this lower valuation if it is enough to cover the amount you want to borrow.

Rent regulation and fair rents

If the landlord is an individual, a non-charitable trust, or a housing co-operative that is not registered with the Housing Corporation (see glossary), then the tenancies are treated as in the private sector, and governed by the Rent Acts.

But if the landlord is either a housing co-operative that is registered with the Housing Corporation, or a housing association, or a charitable trust, any tenancies are treated as in the public sector, and are governed by the Housing Acts.

Under existing legislation most tenants will have the right to a 'fair rent' assessed by the local rent officer. The main exception is where they are a 'co-ownership tenant'. This is where the tenant is entitled under their membership or occupancy agreement ' ... on ceasing to be members ... to a sum calculated by reference directly or indirectly to the value of the dwelling house'.

A rent officer is required to set a fair rent at the hypothetical market rent that would apply if there were no shortage of rented housing in the area. In practice the rent officer compares registered rents in the area in relation to the type and quality of accommodation provided. The rent is fixed for two years, after which a new rent can be registered.

Under the government's proposals most rent controls on new tenancies will be removed. Landlords, including housing associations and co-ops, will let property on assured tenancies or shorthold tenancies. Fair rents will continue to apply to existing tenancies, but will not apply when properties are relet, or on new tenancies.

There will be a limited right for tenants under a shorthold tenancy to have their rent registered by the rent officer, who will be obliged to set it at a market rent, taking into account their lack of security.

Assured tenancies may be for a fixed period, or for a very long term such as 99 years, or they may be periodic.

If an assured tenancy is for a fixed period, it can be continued beyond that period on the same terms until either party gives six months notice of a change. If the new terms, including the rent, cannot be agreed, they can be settled in court on the basis of a market rent.

Very long term assured tenancies would include provisions for a periodic rent review. All the courts will do is ensure that both parties act within the agreed terms of the tenancy.

If an assured tenancy is periodic, such as a weekly or monthly tenancy, a new tenancy automatically applies on the same terms until the tenancy is terminated. Neither party has the right to change the terms except by agreement. Terms would include the basis and the frequency of rent reviews. The courts would only get involved to interpret the terms and ensure both parties acted within them.

Housing Benefit
Housing Benefit is only available to tenants or licensees. Anyone entitled, under their occupancy agreement, to ' . . . a sum calculated by reference directly or indirectly to the value of the dwelling' is regarded as a co-owner, and excluded from Housing Benefit. In which case the DHSS may pay part of their rates and the interest on their share of the mortgage payments if they are unemployed, although under recent legislation this is halved for the first four months.

There are two sorts of Housing Benefit for tenants, with different rules governing the amount you receive. Those who are unemployed receive 'certificated benefit' covering their rent and 80% of their rates. If no fair rent is registered, benefit is paid on the actual rent charged so long as it is not unreasonably high. Under new legislative proposals, the level to which benefit will be paid will be set by the rent officer.

Those who are employed but on low incomes may qualify for 'standard benefit',which is earnings-related. Those on the lowest incomes receive payment covering the whole of their rent and 80% of their rates. As income rises the proportion of their rent and rates covered by the benefit rapidly tapers off.

Leaflets explaining your entitlement should be available from most post offices, your local DHSS, and the local authority housing department.

CHAPTER 4

Joint ownership through a trust

How a joint ownership trust works

It is common enough for two people to share the ownership of a house. Both names go on the title deeds of the property. Many married people jointly own their homes in this way. Wherever two or more people who are not married share ownership of a house the arrangements between them can get a little complicated, and it is better to be more precise about them. The way to do this is through a 'trust deed'.

This chapter describes a particular form of trust, in which any number of people can share the ownership of a property, including the right to sell their share of the property when they leave. Essentially a trust is a body governed by a trust deed which defines the relationship between the 'trustees' and the 'beneficiaries'. In a joint-ownership trust these are the same people, and you never see the terms mentioned. Instead they are referred to as 'parties' to the trust agreement.

It does not much matter how many of the trustees' names are registered with the title deeds of the property (the legal maximum is four), because the trust deed redefines all their rights and responsibilities as owners so as to share them amongst all the parties.

This form of trust is very flexible, and can even be used where the property is already owned by one or more of the people concerned, in which case the building society need not even know about it.

Other types of trust

Under the type of trust described in this chapter the parties are effectively all joint owners of the property, with all the benefits normally available to an individual home owner, including their entitlement to full share of any increase in the value of the property when they leave.

However, it is possible to set up a trust where the trustees own the property but nobody can take out any share of the increase in value when they leave. The trustees need to be living in the property as their main residence in order for the trust as a whole to qualify for many benefits of home ownership. But these benefits are held in trust on behalf of present and future residents of the property. The people living in the property will be more like tenants than joint owners.

Unless the trust is registered as a charity, so that the rights of the trustees are legally bound by its charitable purposes, it is hard to ensure that the trustees at any point in time do not sell up and pocket the profits, having paid off the outstanding loan. This would be unfair if other people had contributed to the mortgage payments on the understanding that the trustees would not profit from the increase in the value of the property.

Trustees will have to show that they are making no profit from the rent in order to avoid being taxed on it as part of their personal income. They could be liable to pay Capital Gains Tax if the property were ever sold or transferred to another organisation, unless they can show that it was the trustees' main place of residence throughout the period they were the registered owners of the property. Each trustee can have one dwelling exempted in this way.

Anyone paying rent to live in the property who was not a trustee and had no stake in the value of the property would be a tenant. Such tenancies would be regulated by the Rent Acts, and be subject to rent control as well as limits on the trustee' right to evict.

Generally speaking, a housing co-operative is better suited to forms of shared ownership in which people live in the property as tenants other than on a temporary basis.

The trust deed

The trust deed in Appendix A was first developed by a solicitor in order jointly to own his house with some friends. He has since adapted and developed it over several years for use by a large number of groups of 'joint owners'.

The deed starts by naming the 'parties' to the agreement and explaining, under 'recitals' who they are and what they are agreeing to. There is no limit to the number of people included as 'parties' to the agreement, though it is doubtful whether a trust is the most appropriate legal form for a group of more than half a dozen.

In the sample deed in the appendix persons A, B and C are the registered owners on the title deeds, with person D sharing in the property solely through the trust deed.

By this arrangement. although only a limited number of people appear on the title and mortgage agreement and are themselves owners, others can live with them and share in the ownership and responsibility for the mortgage, repairs, and so on, under the terms of the trust deed.

Shares in the property

The proportions in which the individuals own shares of the property form the basis on which all common bills, such as those for maintenance or rates, are shared out.

It is simplest to hold equal shares in the property, and divide the common bills equally between you. You may decide to go further and share out the bills so as to take some account of different income levels within the group. But you would not write something of that nature into the trust deed, which has to define the position you would retreat to if you were unable to reach agreement amongst yourselves.

There are circumstances under which you might choose to own different proportions of the property, such as where it is divided into relatively self-contained units. In this case it could make more sense to own shares of the property related to the value of each separate unit. You might be better off with a leasehold arrangement under these circumstances, provided you could raise mortgage loans against the value of each separate unit. This is discussed in the next chapter.

Another reason for holding unequal shares could be that you wish to have someone living with you who could not afford to buy an equal share of the property, either because they did not have the cash for their share of the deposit, or could not afford the mortgage payments, or both.

Social problems can arise wherever you introduce inequalities, and you should carefully consider the consequences. It is especially difficult if people live at different standards within the same household. Make it clear that each person has an equal say in making decisions, no matter what proportion of the property they own, or how long they have been in the group. Be explicit about those things that are unequal, and take positive steps to encourage equal participation in every other way.

The mortgage
You don't necessarily have a share in the mortgage in the same proportions as your share of the house. Some can pay more of the costs of buying and setting up the property in cash and others through the mortgage.

So while all other expenses are paid according to the proportions in which you share in the property, each person's liabilities for mortgage payments are defined as a separate percentage of the amount due on the mortgage.

Repairs
Shared property may be particularly vulnerable to deterioration through lack of maintenance. It can be hard to get everyone to agree to take on a repair at any particular time, when some of them might be short of money, or have other priorities. In this deed the advantage is given to those in favour of getting the work done. Any party has the right to repair the

property to adequate standards. If they cannot agree on the need for work to be done a chartered surveyor is appointed to arbitrate.

Everyone contributes to the cost of repair and general maintenance of the buildings, together with the costs of agreed improvements. These are shared out in the proportions mentioned above.

Some groups prefer to make regular payments into an accumulating maintenance fund, to ensure there is money to keep the property in good repair. This could be written into the deed, or done by mutual agreement. Often people buying property are fully stretched financially at that time and prefer to delay the extra commitment.

Personal areas
Each member of the group can have their own personal area within the property defined in the deed. This might be just one or two bedrooms, but could include a whole suite of rooms. If most of the property is divided up so as to give self-contained units, you should consider whether separate leases would be more appropriate.

Try to avoid defining in the deed arrangements that are likely to change. If you are each occupying one floor of a four-storey house and sharing the ground floor and garden, it is probably best to say so in the deed. But if you each have a bedroom in an otherwise shared house, it is likely you will swap rooms from time to time, in which case there is not much point in defining the arrangement.

There is also provision in the deed for sub-letting. If this increases the number of people using the shared areas, a part of the rent you receive goes to the rest of the group. But if you are allowing someone else to use your part of the house while you take a world cruise, you keep all the proceeds. You cannot create a tenancy, giving someone else the right to live in the house, without the agreement of everyone else in the group.

Handling the payments
The deed provides for setting up a joint bank account to pay all the bills. If anyone fails to pay their share of the costs the others can charge them interest on the amount owed. If they have let their part of the house and gone away, the others can collect the rent to meet their share of the payments.

In practice some groups pay all their bills individually without using the joint account. So long as the bills get paid on time this arrangement can be satisfactory. The provisions in the deed then provide a safety net to ensure that if any members of the group are unhappy with the individual arrangements they can insist they all set up a joint account and pay together.

Restrictions
Without restrictions in the deed other members of the group would have no say in whether anyone could keep a pack of afghan hounds in their bedroom or run a mail-order business shipping out five hundred carpets a week. So the agreement says you cannot keep pets or run a business, which does not stop you agreeing to be more flexible, and only objecting where it would cause you problems. You might agree to 'turn a blind eye' to something for a while to see how it went. Once you agree to waive a restriction you lose the right to re-impose it. It is safer to agree in writing to make an exception, specifying the circumstances under which you have a right to revoke it.

Sale
Any legal agreement to share property has to provide a balance between the rights of the individual and those of the rest of the group. The ultimate assurance

for the individual is their right to leave if the arrangements no longer suit them. Most of the rest of the
deed concerns the right of anyone to leave and sell
their share of the property. Having clear agreements
on handling someone's departure reduces mis-
understandings as well as your dependence on good-
will, which in practice can enable departures to
proceed more harmoniously.

Those remaining have the right to buy them out, or
to find someone else to replace them. If they cannot
agree on a price the whole property is valued and
their share is worked out on the basis of the proportion they own, as mentioned earlier under 'shares
in the property'.

It is important to have time limits for each stage of
this process. At any point you can agree to waive
them. In practice there is usually some slippage, and
with the best will in the world it can take months to
settle. The deed allows seven months for those remaining to find a way of replacing the one who wants
to leave. They can buy them out either individually or
together. Or they can find someone else to take their
place. If they are unwilling or unable to do it in that
time, the one who wants to go can force the sale of
the property. To avoid disputes over its value it is
sold at auction as quickly as possible and the trust is
wound up.

Another possibility is the situation of everyone
agreeing they want to end the agreement, but being
unable to decide who should buy out whom. The
deed then allows for the 'drawing of lots' to determine the issue. Once again, if this should arise there
is nothing to prevent you reaching an agreement
based on more appropriate criteria. The purpose of
this clause is to ensure a means of resolving the
conflict without dragging each other through the
courts.

Making changes
The trust deed in Appendix A could provide the basis
for discussions between you on what you want. You
may require additions to it, or to delete parts that are
not right for your group. Once you are clear about
what you want, your solicitor can draw up a deed to
suit your requirements.

It is quite simple to change a trust deed. You draw
up an agreement specifying the change for all the
parties to sign. This is known as a 'supplementary
deed'. If you are making major changes, you could
draw up a completely new one stating that it super-
sedes the old deed. All that is required is that you all
sign it.

If you are changing the 'parties' to the agreement,
the change must be signed by the departing parties as
well as by any ones to be added.

It is worth checking out any changes with your
solicitor, because small changes could have big re-
sults. The law on housing can get very complicated.
In a few cases the lender may insist on a clause in the
mortgage agreement requiring the lender's approval
before any change is made in the trust agreement.

The possibility of waiving restrictions, or being
more generous in your dealings with each other has
been mentioned a few times. The deed has to set out
what you will do in ways that are workable even if
you are at loggerheads with each other. It has to
consider the 'worst case'. Most of the time you will
want to do a great deal better than that in your dealings with one another.

It is a matter for careful judgement to decide
whether to enshrine the way you work in practice in a
new or supplementary deed. If everyone's expec-
tations of each other are very different from those in
your legal agreement, you could be in for a shock if a
serious conflict arose. At that point what is written in
the deed will take precedence over anything you

have said or done in practice.

Other considerations

What about tax relief?

Home owners get tax relief on the interest element of their mortgage repayments. Under the MIRAS scheme the subsidy is claimed for you by the building society or bank that gives you the loan. This is explained in chapter 2 (page 20). It does not matter how many joint owners there are or whether all their names are on the mortgage agreement – the payments will automatically be adjusted by the tax relief subsidy. Each person is entitled to relief on a loan of up to £30,000 (in 1987). Until the regulations are changed, four joint owners would be entitled to tax relief on £120,000, except that a married couple would count as one. It is not clear whether it would be possible to raise the limit to take account of those who had not signed the mortgage agreement, and whose names did not appear on the title deeds.

What about Housing Benefit?

The Housing Benefit regulations distinguish between owners and tenants. Owners do not qualify for Housing Benefit. They may receive assistance from the DHSS with their rates and the interest payments on their mortgage. Under recent changes in the rules, this assistance is halved for the first four months they are unemployed or on supplementary benefit. In the early years of a conventional annuity mortgage most of the payments are of interest, and would be covered.

Tenants qualify for Housing Benefit if they are unemployed, and can also qualify on the grounds of low income.

Under a joint ownership arrangement you would be treated as owners. There is no way that anyone entitled to a share in the value of the property could qualify for Housing Benefit as a tenant.

Creating a tenancy

If you want others living with you who are not parties to the trust deed, or if you sub-let your part of the property for any reason, you may be creating a tenancy. There are some guidelines in chapter 3 on ways of ensuring you do not unintentionally create a secure or 'protected' tenancy. The most relevant of these is likely to be the exemption granted on tenancies where the landlord's principle home is in the same house.

Think carefully about the consequences of having two classes of people living in the same house: the owners with a financial stake in the value of the property, and the tenants, who could lose their home if the owners ever decided to sell up.

Your mortgage will almost certainly prohibit you from letting any part of the property to a tenant. This is true for most home owners, though some of them choose to ignore it. As far as the lender is concerned, a tenancy you create is not secure so long as they have not acknowledged it. They can evict anyone to obtain vacant possession if you breach the terms of the mortgage agreement. So in practice they will not be too bothered if you do let to a tenant.

Anyone occupying the property who has not signed the mortgage agreement may be required by the lender to sign a form of consent to the mortgage, in which they acknowledge that any rights they may have are subject to the superior rights of the lender under the terms of the mortgage agreement.

Anyone with a stake in the value of the property will be an owner, not a tenant. This would apply to everyone who had signed as a party to a trust deed like the one in Appendix A. They would have no rights under the Rent Acts either to a fair rent or to protect them from eviction — their rights would be governed simply by their own trust agreement.

Raising the money for joint ownership in a trust

Banks and building societies are much less restrictive than they used to be in deciding to whom they are prepared to lend. If there are more people chasing mortgages than there is money available, they tend to become that bit more conservative and go for the happily married couple you see in the advertisements. Much of the time, however, they are seeking to expand their share of the loan market, and it is in their interests to draw more people into home ownership.

Most lending bodies rely on the word of your solicitor, who is obliged by professional ethics to inform them of anything that compromises the terms of their mortgage agreement. Your solicitor will usually help you approach likely lenders. Most mortgage managers will not be concerned to enquire any further than the financial status of the persons named on the mortgage agreement, so long as your solicitor assures them that sensible arrangements have been made between the joint owners.

The lender's concerns are covered by the mortgage agreement. The trust agreement merely creates a second set of responsibilities between those who signed the mortgage and any others living in the property, and need be of no concern to a lender.

If your solicitor has experience of setting up trusts like yours they will know which institutions are likely to respond positively. The Abbey National, the Halifax and the National Westminster Bank's home loans scheme have all supported trusts based on the deed in Appendix A.

When there is a shortage of mortgage funds, priority is sometimes given to people who have savings

with a society. If any of you have savings with a
building society it is worth approaching them at an
early stage. If they refuse to lend on a joint ownership scheme, you could move your money to one that
is more sympathetic. Most banks also have home
loan schemes, so talk to your local manager.

Raising the money to buy out someone leaving

In practice most trusts are small, involving three or
four friends sharing a house. One or two may have a
bit of capital but not enough income to support a
mortgage, while the others have the income but not
enough cash for the deposit. Together they can afford
to buy the sort of property they want. The deed
allows for these differences.

When one of them wants to leave, the others
usually buy them out. In this way most end up as
fairly conventional family households. Sometimes
another person comes in to buy out the one leaving,
and occasionally a property is divided into two or
more self-contained flats, which can be sold off separately when necessary.

If those remaining cannot afford to buy them out,
or find a suitable replacement, the whole arrangement is terminated with the sale of the house and
distribution of the proceeds.

Building societies are used to the situation where
two people who jointly own a house split up. They
will usually remortgage the property so that the one
who remains can buy out the one leaving with the aid
of a larger mortgage loan. Their only concerns are
that the remaining borrower's income is sufficient to
cover the mortgage payments, and that the current
value of the property provides sufficient security to
cover the larger loan.

The problem for joint owners in a trust is similar.
Anyone buying out the share of someone leaving is

likely to need to borrow the money. The person going will want their share of the value of the property, less their share of the mortgage loan outstanding.

If the house has not increased in value in the meantime, the only cash they will take is the money they put in in the first place, and it should be a relatively simple matter to transfer their share of the mortgage loan to another person. If the house is worth a great deal more than they originally paid for it, the person leaving will want their share of this increased value in cash when they sell their share of the property. In most cases the only way to raise it is by remortgaging the property.

Many building societies are reluctant to lend to trusts because of this implied liability to remortgage the property whenever someone wants to leave. They are worried about the administrative costs and complications. It is all a question of how often they reckon it will arise. First-time buyers, however, often move to larger houses after two or three years, which is much more expensive for everyone concerned than remortgaging a house. In practice changes of ownership in trusts do not seem to be any more frequent.

Fortunately there are banks and building societies who accept this. It might be worth checking the conditions under which they would be prepared to remortgage to help you replace someone leaving. Otherwise you could all find yourselves having to sell up when one wanted to go. Even if you do not get a commitment to remortgage under these circumstances, the lender should be able to give you some idea of the criteria they would apply. Be careful not to give the impression that it will happen frequently.

You should discuss the implications of this between yourselves, bearing in mind the right of the person leaving to sell their share of the property. If you cannot be sure of raising the money to buy them out yourselves, or of replacing them with someone who could buy their share, you have to accept the prospect of selling up and going your separate ways.

CHAPTER 5

Leasehold

99 YEAR LEASE

EACH HOUSEHOLDER OWNS A LONG LEASE
ON THEIR OWN SELF-CONTAINED UNIT.

How leasehold works

This chapter examines arrangements under which
each householder owns a long lease on their own
self-contained unit or flat. When the lease expires
after 99 years or more, ownership of the flat reverts to
the freeholder. The cost of maintaining the common
parts and structure of the building is collected from

the leaseholders through a service charge which will go up and down with the costs. In addition, the leaseholder pays a ground rent to the freeholder.

These self-contained units are usually within a larger building or complex of buildings, or part of a house that has been divided into separate flats.

The leaseholder's relationship with the freeholder is defined in the lease agreement. The freehold will be worth very little money, because most of the value of the building has been transferred to the leases. A leaseholder 'owns' their flat, and can raise a mortgage on it in just the same way as any other householder.

The first part of this chapter describes the practicalities of sharing ownership of the freehold. It then goes on to look at how this could be used by a group of people to buy a property and share it so that each of them owns a lease on their private unit; or by leaseholders who want to take over the freehold of the mansion block in which they already own their own flats.

The freehold

In the commercial development of flats the freehold is often sold off by the developer, sometimes to a local estate agent, and will only fetch four or five times the value of the ground rents paid under the terms of the leases. A typical ground rent will be between £50 and £150 a year, so that the freehold of a small block of three flats is unlikely to be worth more than £2000. This ground rent goes straight to the freeholder.

Although it may not be worth much, the freehold is very important. In England and Wales the best way to manage the common services is for the freeholder to be responsible for them. These would include maintenance of the corridors and stairs, and of the structural fabric of the building, as well as ensuring the other leaseholders keep within the terms of their leases and do not cause a nuisance to their neighbours. It is vital that the freehold is owned in a way that facilitates this.

The freeholder will have certain powers under the lease agreements. A leaseholder will have to obtain their written approval before making alterations or extensions to the building that might effect the other leaseholders.

The obligations of the freeholder are defined in the lease agreements made with each leaseholder. It would make management of the freehold simplest if these were essentially the same on each lease, although there is no legal reason why they should not vary from flat to flat.

Joint ownership of the freehold

Up to four people can own the freehold (except in Scotland where there is no limit). It would be up to them to agree how best to carry out their responsibilities. If these involve little more than maintaining the structure and external fabric of the building, the freeholders may be able to meet from time to time to deal with matters that arise without the need for any formal rules or procedures.

But if the freeholders provide a wider range of services, such as maintaining lifts and communal spaces, cleaning corridors, and looking after the grounds, it might be better to have a written agreement on how they jointly manage their responsibilities.

Where the benefits of owning the freehold are minimal, and the responsibilities not onerous, the simplest way of sharing the freehold may still be to have four names on the title deeds. The costs of maintaining the fabric of the building would be shared by the leaseholders under the terms of their lease agreements.

There are two reasons for setting up an organisation to own or manage the freehold: there may be more than four leaseholders who want to share the benefits and responsibilities equally between them; or because the freeholders' rights and responsibilities are complicated and you wish to set up an appropriate framework within which to share them. In which case you could choose to form:

- a trust to manage the freehold, with up to four names on the title deeds of the freehold, sharing rights and responsibilities with all parties under the terms of the the trust agreement. Your solicitor should be able to draw up a suitable agreement for you;
- a leasehold co-ownership association as described in the next chapter; or
- a management company as described below.

Forming a company to own the freehold

The most common way to handle joint ownership of the freehold is to create a company with 100 shares and divide them equally between the leaseholders. The company owns the freehold, but the leaseholders own the company through their shares. The leaseholders will make themselves the company's directors and any disagreement will be settled by vote.

This has a number of advantages:

- It gives every leaseholder a vote on decisions affecting the management of the freehold;
- It can be used for any size of scheme as there is no limit to the number of shareholders − there may be just two of them; whereas you cannot have more than four people's names directly on the title deeds of the freehold (except in Scotland), and you need seven to form a co-ownership;
- It is relatively cheap to set up, costing between £200 and £300;

- It saves money when someone moves on. If each individual has their name on the title deeds of the freehold, this has to be changed every time a flat is sold, which is unnecessarily complicated and expensive. Transferring their shares to the new owner involves no more than signing a share transfer;
- It is familiar to lawyers so the leaseholder will not have to spend a long time explaining the set-up to someone purchasing their flat, and people buying will not have problems explaining it to their building society;
- It is subject to less bureaucratic interference than a co-ownership, though you do have to have your annual accounts audited and submit annual returns to the Registrar of Companies, together with a 'filing fee' (£20 a year at 1987 prices).

If all you want it for is to manage the freehold, forming a company in which each leaseholder owns an equal share could be the simplest solution.

Before forming a management company, there are some disadvantages that you should consider in case they could affect you.

If the company borrows money to buy the freehold or to do major repairs or renovation to the property, you would not be eligible for tax relief on the interest. The leaseholders would be eligible if they raised the money individually for repairs to their own unit. But if you need to raise loans collectively you should consider one of the other ways of sharing ownership of the freehold.

If the company ever sold the freehold or transferred it to another organisation it could be liable to pay tax on any increase in its value. It could also be taxed on the surplus it makes in any year out of the rents charged to leaseholders, even though these might be intended to build up a reserve out of which to tackle some major roof repair, for example.

BYHWOP—E

Most company profits are taxable, even where they arise purely out of the contributions of the members of your group. For example, repayment of a loan to the company out of rents charged under the terms of your leases would reduce the debts of the company, which would be shown as a profit on the company's balance sheet.

If you are using the company to make repairs and improvements to the flats before selling long leases on them to yourselves, you could miss the opportunity to qualify for Repair Grants and Improvement Grants. These are sometimes available to home owners, and to those who provide accommodation for rent (see chapter 2, page 31). They are not available to companies that sell leases on their property.

Although it is relatively simple to buy an 'off the shelf' company and set it up yourself, there are potential complications, some of which are mentioned above. So it is wise to go to a solicitor who understands the complexities of housing law and be sure to follow their advice.

The leases

Leases can get very complicated. They must be marketable and meet building society requirements to ensure the buyer can raise a mortgage loan on them. For this reason it is best to leave any non-essential agreements between you to a separate agreement, particularly if they might make the lease harder to sell, or harder to explain to the purchaser's solicitor.

Leasehold is very common. Virtually every owner-occupied flat in England and Wales is sold on a lease, and there is no reason why your use of it should not be entirely conventional. The lease defines the relationship between the leaseholder and the freeholder. If all the property is divided up between the leaseholders on long leases, the freehold will not be worth much, and there could be precious little advantage in having your names on it.

The responsibilities of the freeholder usually include repairing the roof and foundations, and the exterior upkeep of the building. Any leaseholder can require the freeholder to carry out their duties, which might include such things as ensuring that other leaseholders obey any restrictions in their leases on the keeping of pets or causing of nuisance.

The lease defines what payments the leaseholder must make to the freeholder which may include a ground rent, and a regular service charge to cover the cost of the services provided. It will also include obligations to pay a proportion of the costs of all repairs that are not the responsibility of individual leaseholders.

Buying a property and dividing it up with separate leases

The freehold is bought jointly, usually in the names of all the joint owners (up to a legal maximum of four). The property is then divided up giving each member of the group a lease on a self-contained unit.

You will probably choose not to put a fence around each person's separate part of the garden, and may well share other facilities both inside and outside the house. The principle underlying this approach is that the total value of the property is transferred to long leases leaving the freehold practically worthless. You can then individually raise mortgages on your part of the property.

If one of you wishes to leave they can sell their unit. If you have an 'option agreement' those remaining either have the right to buy them out at valuation or more commonly, have first refusal on any sale: if they can match any other buyer's price they have first option to purchase. This additional agreement can, at any time, be registered on the title to the property. Most don't bother to do this because it is so unlikely any sale could take place without you noticing it. If in doubt, it is safest to register it.

A typical example of the use of this approach might be where a couple and a friend wanted to buy a big house and divide it into two flats, sharing the garden, the garage and a workshop, together with a dark-room and laundry in the basement.

The couple take a lease in both their names on the upper two floors which are converted to a self-contained unit, with a fire escape that effectively gives them access to the garden. The left side of the garden is theirs, together with the garage. The ground floor including the hallway and basement becomes their friend's, who also gains the right-hand side of the garden and the workshop attached to the garage. The couple may have rights of access through the front door, hall and stairs, but in every other respect the property is divided into two self-contained units, with access to the upper flat via the fire escape.

If the friend downstairs ever sold up the couple would prefer to buy them out. But if they were unable to do that or to find anyone else who wanted to share with them in a similar way, they could run a fence down the middle of the garden and it would be sold as a separate self-contained unit.

Numerous variations are possible, so long as you do not compromise the value of each separate unit as far as the mortgage lender is concerned.

In practice there might be others living in the house whom the building society knows nothing about. So long as the lender does not acknowledge the existence of a tenancy created after the mortgage is contracted, their right to vacant possession if the mortgage agreement is breached will not be compromised.

If you are planning to have people living in the

house whose names do not appear on any title deed, you should consider whether you might be better off with a trust agreement. A trust provides more scope for defining everybodies' rights and responsibilities, particularly where they are to share in the value of the property as joint owners.

How to raise the money
Each leaseholder raises their own mortgage loan secured against the value of their lease. This is generally easier than raising a mortgage on a shared house, because each unit can be sold separately.

So long as the value of the lease is sufficient security for the loan you require, and you are earning enough to support the mortgage payments, it should be no harder raising a mortgage on your lease than on any other kind of property.

If you are converting or renovating a property, you would raise a bridging loan for which you would share liability. This is usually arranged through a bank. They will be concerned that the value of the property at all stages of the development process is sufficient to cover the loan they are making on it. If not, they will require some other form of security, such as a guarantee from someone else with property that they will pay the money back if you are unable to do so.

If you are doing the renovation work yourselves or expect to take a long time over it for any other reason, you might consider forming a trust to jointly own the property while you convert it. This would be much the same as the trust described in chapter 4. If there are more than half a dozen of you doing the conversion work yourselves there are advantages in forming a leasehold co-ownership, as described in the next chapter.

Joining together to buy the freehold

It sometimes occurs to flat owners that the freeholder is charging an unreasonable amount for the meagre service provided. Or they may have complaints about the quality of work done, and the speed at which repairs are dealt with. In that case, they may succeed in reaching agreement with those who own the other flats in the building to buy the freehold jointly, and to share the freeholder's responsibilities and costs between them.

The simplest way of doing this is to form a management company with each leaseholder owning equal shares. Their shares would be sold with the lease to anyone who bought the flat.

The money to purchase the shares in the management company would be raised by the individual leaseholders. Usually the freehold is not worth much; if it is, they might be able to remortgage their flat for a larger loan based on the additional value of owning a share of the freehold.

This solution works well so long as you are not borrowing money through the company to buy the freehold or any other property, or to do repairs and alterations to the building. In which case you could be at a double disadvantage: you could lose out on the tax relief normally available on the interest on the loan, and you could also lose the opportunity for Repair or Improvement Grants. (see chapter 2, page 29).

If, however, you have already borrowed up to the limit for tax relief on a mortgage loan (£30,000 in 1987) and the local authority is not making any of the grants available, these disadvantages would be immaterial.

If any of these considerations apply to you, you should consider forming a leasehold co-ownership as described in the next chapter.

CHAPTER 6

Co-ownerships

DEPARTING TENANTS RECEIVE PAYMENT BASED ON INCREASE IN THE VALUE OF THE PROPERTY.

What is a co-ownership society?

A co-ownership society is a housing association in which the members have a stake in the value of the houses they occupy, so that they have most of the benefits of owner occupiers.

In the schemes we have described so far the property was owned by the people living in it, and the

71

agreements describing how they shared the rights and responsibilities of ownership were private documents drawn up for them by their solicitor. A co-ownership society is a very different kind of legal form. It has a life of its own and is registered as a housing association with the Registrar of Friendly Societies.

The society owns property and pays taxes just like a person. In the legal jargon, it is a 'corporate body' and has 'limited liability' for its debts, signified by 'Limited' or 'Ltd' after its name.

The members each hold one share in the association, which is normally for a nominal amount, such as £1 or £5. They all have an equal say in managing the co-ownership.

Co-ownership Societies are similar to housing co-operatives except that the tenants receive a payment when they leave based on any increase in the value of their share of the property. In this way they are much more like owners than tenants.

There have been a variety of co-ownership schemes over the last 20 years, mostly aimed at providing a form of home ownership to people who might otherwise have been unable to obtain a mortgage. Most of those set up in the sixties and early seventies, using a combination of building society mortgages and government grants, were dissolved following the 'power to sell' in the 1980 Housing Act, with the houses sold to their tenants for the value of the outstanding debt on them.

Nowadays the needs of those who could not otherwise afford to buy are more often met through 'shared ownership' schemes, under which they buy as much of the house as they can afford and rent the rest. These are described in chapter 8. The Housing Corporation has published a leaflet explaining how they work, and can put you in touch with housing associations providing this route to owning a home of your own.

Coventry Churches Housing Association is still developing co-ownership housing, designed to meet the special needs of the elderly. Their 'Sundowner' scheme is now being promoted by the Housing Corporation, and is also described briefly below.

In most of these early schemes the reasons for sharing ownership were purely economic, and the relations between people within the co-ownership were much the same as between neighbours on any housing estate. They were managed through a committee of tenants, but the work was done by professional housing managers through the parent housing association.

The co-ownership model was also used by those who wanted to create a sense of community with their housing, whilst retaining a good degree of privacy and most of the advantages of home ownership. It has the flexibility to provide for both.

How does a co-ownership society work?

The National Federation of Housing Associations (NFHA) has produced sets of 'model rules' developed specifically for co-ownership societies. The simplest way to set up is to register through the NFHA.

The sample rules for a housing co-operative in Appendix B could also be used for a co-ownership . Co-ownerships are a form of housing co-operative. Housing co-op rules are suitable for co-ownerships, provided that:

- The rules restrict membership to tenants or prospective tenants, and preclude the granting of tenancies to anyone who is not a member of the co-operative (for example, see rules 2a and 9a in Appendix B); and
- The rules on 'Application of Profits' allow for payment to be made to a member when they leave so

that they can receive their share in the value of the house they have occupied (for example, see rule 16a in Appendix B).

In other words, what you require is rules for a 'fully mutual', 'equity sharing' housing co-operative. There is just one problem with being fully mutual: to form a housing co-operative or any sort of housing association you have to have at least seven members. If you never expect to grow and to have more than half a dozen or so in your group, you should consider forming a trust (see chapter 4) or using a leasehold arrangement like those described in chapter 5.

The Empty Property Unit (EPU) at Shelter and the National Federation of Housing Co-operatives (NFHC) have developed rules for 'fully mutual' housing co-operatives that are suitable for co-ownerships. You can also register through them.

The other thing you will need is a lease or occupancy agreement defining for each person living in the property what their rights and responsibilities are. This is where their right to a share in the value of the property is specified.

The exact form of this will vary according to which type of co-ownership you require.

Different types of co-ownership
There are three forms of co-ownership currently in use. All offer their members a stake in the value of the property, but they differ in the way in which they are financed.

In the first form, each household raises a mortgage on their own unit which they buy from the co-ownership association under a very long lease, in much the same way as under the leasehold arrangement described in the previous chapter. This we shall refer to as a 'leasehold co-ownership'.

In the second form, the co-ownership association is set up and professionally managed by a parent housing association. They raise one mortgage for the whole scheme, which is then paid for out of the rents collected on each separate unit. The 'Sundowner' model described below is of this type.

The third form is similar to the trust arrangements described in chapter 4, in which the members of the co-ownership buy a property with one mortgage on the property as a whole, which they pay for out of their rents. We describe these as 'self help co-ownerships' to distinguish them from those managed by a parent body.

Leasehold co-ownership

Why form a leasehold co-ownership?
Leasehold co-ownership could be used by tenants to take over a large mansion block. The co-ownership buys the freehold. If the property requires renovation, the co-owners would use architects to draw up and cost out the complete scheme, and then get a qualified valuer to assess the value of each renovated unit.

The purchase and development costs are shared between the flats on the basis of their valuation. This determines the price each occupant pays to purchase a 99-year lease on their unit.

In practice it can be difficult to purchase and renovate a block of flats without spending more than they will be valued at when completed. There are a number of ways you might be able to reduce the costs:

- If they have security of tenure, tenants should be able to buy the houses they are living in for considerably less than they would be worth as vacant property.
- You may be eligible for Improvement Grants (see chapter 2, page 31). These are mostly discretionary, and their availability will depend on how much money the local authority has to spend.

- You may be able to do some of the renovation work yourselves. The Housing Corporation has a scheme under which it can provide special help to groups of people doing 'self-build rehabilitation', including helping them to borrow the money to finance the development of the property.

In some cases, the tenants may take over the block of flats without doing any immediate renovation. In which case the problem is reduced to ensuring that each occupant can raise sufficient money with a mortgage to buy their flat.

A leaseholder is unlikely to be able to borrow more than 85% or 90% of the valuation of their unit with a mortgage loan. They have to provide the remainder as a deposit in cash, either from their own savings, or by borrowing from relatives or friends. They also have to be able to afford the mortgage repayments.

There are a variety of other situations in which leasehold co-ownership can be relevant. It can be used, for instance, by people who already own the leases on their flats in order to take over the freehold of the whole block and manage it themselves. They may have to remortgage their individual units to raise the cash for their share of the cost of buying the freehold, and of any repairs or improvements they wish to carry out at the time. They might, for example, want to make entry to the block more secure, with entry phones and a locked main entrance.

This form of co-ownership has also been used to buy large rural houses and covert them into self contained flats which are then bought on 99-year leases by their new occupants. The co-ownership retains the grounds and some outbuildings, which it manages for the benefit of all the leaseholders. A leaseholder's right of access to any such shared facilities enhances the value of their lease.

How does leasehold co-ownership work?

This solution operates very much like the leasehold arrangement described in chapter 5. A large property is bought and converted into separate units. Each household buys a long lease (99 years is common), with a mortgage loan secured on the value of their unit. They also become members of the co-ownership housing association and share the rights and responsibilities of the freehold.

When a leaseholder wants to leave they put their unit onto the market and whoever they sell it to replaces them as a member of the association. The extent to which the association has any say in selecting people who move into the property varies from scheme to scheme. In practice, the association usually arranges the sale, with the proceeds (less legal costs) going to the seller. In some cases the leaseholder is responsible for finding a buyer, with the association having a limited right to object to anyone that refuses to abide by their democratic procedures.

Under this approach virtually all the value of the property is transferred from the freehold to the separate leases, leaving it up to the individual households to raise however much they need to cover the cost of their unit. So long as the cost of buying and converting the property can be recouped from the sale of the separate leases, there is no need for the co-ownership association to do more than raise bridging loans until the renovation is completed.

The scheme allows some flexibility, in that the co-ownership association can retain, for example, some or all of the land in a rural scheme, and develop common facilities for the mutual benefit of its members. Loans used for this purpose can be eligible for tax relief in the same way as for owner occupiers, so long as the loans are 'for the purchase or improvement of property for occupation by members'. This could, for example, include common dining facilities, creche facilities, meeting rooms, and a variety of other possibilities to enrich the lives of your members and create a sense of community.

This way of developing housing with a degree of community sharing is more common in some countries than it is in Britain, for instance in New Zealand, Denmark and Holland. Success depends on finding a group of people with the capability to set up the association, and to raise the necessary bridging loans to buy and renovate the property. This requires a certain degree of skill and a great deal of patience. Those that have been set up in this country have been very successful, with no reports of difficulties replacing people wanting to leave.

Financing a leasehold co-ownership

You may be buying a block of flats you already occupy, or be buying a large property and dividing it into separate units, very like a property developer. Alternatively you might buy a site and build from scratch, or purchase a property that has already been converted to self-contained units, but needs some renovation.

The principle is that the income from the sale of long leases on the separate units should be sufficient to finance all the costs of setting up the co-ownership, and purchasing and developing the housing. For this to work, the total valuation of all the separate units needs to exceed the cost of purchase and development by a margin sufficient to cover all the incidental legal and administrative costs.

In addition to the separate leases there may be common areas, which might include the grounds and some shared facilities within the buildings. The provision to the leaseholders of rights of access and use of these facilities may enhance the value of their leases, so that even though this part of the property is not divided up, it contributes to the total valuation.

Once the leases are sold to the members, the association continues to manage the freehold and the common parts, and may act as a forum through which the members can develop their common interests; but it no longer has a role in financing the property.

Each household raises their own mortgage against the security of their lease. This is the same arrangement as for anyone buying a long lease on a flat, and should create no special problems for a lender, so long as the valuation provides sufficient security for the loan. As with most people buying a dwelling, the mortgage is unlikely to cover 100% of the purchase price, and you will have to find the rest from your own resources. The amount of deposit you will need could be increased if the valuation of your unit is less than the cost of it.

Financing the development phase
Financing a leasehold co-ownership is generally simpler than the other forms of co-ownership because the mortgage loans are raised individually by each leaseholder against the value of their lease.

But it will not be possible to raise mortgage loans on leases on the separate units until they are completed. If you are taking on an existing block of flats and can move in immediately this will not be much of a problem. But if you are doing extensive renovation work, or building from scratch, you will need to finance the development phase. This is usually done with bank loans.

Raising bridging loans can be quite difficult. There may be phases of development in which the property is worth less than you will have spent on it, so that it no longer provides adequate security for the loan. The Housing Corporation may be able to put you in touch with a secondary co-operative or housing association working with housing co-operatives in your area who could help you through the development phase.

If you are doing most of the renovation work your-selves you could qualify for help from the Housing Corporation under their Self-Build Rehabilitation scheme. They may be able to help you finance the development phase, and in a number of other ways.

If the co-ownership, as opposed to the individual leaseholders, needs to borrow money for any reason, you should read the advice on financing a co-ownership through the rents (see page 84). If you are doing the conversions yourselves you might start off with one mortgage on the property as a whole until the renovation work is completed.

Co-ownerships set up by parent housing associations

Coventry Churches Housing Association has deve-loped a number of schemes using building society finance to provide housing for those who seek the benefits of home ownership without the means to secure it. Andrew Thomas has written about them in his book 'New Homes for Old' (see bibliography).

These schemes include the Sundowner package, which involves setting up a co-ownership association to buy land and build housing designed to meet the particular needs of the elderly, using a 100% mort-gage from a building society.

Old people sometimes find themselves in posses-sion of unsuitable housing without the means to convert it or to buy something more appropriate. They need someone who can keep a look-out in case they are suddenly ill, or an alarm system linked to a neighbour, or a warden.

How does Sundowner work?
If a member wishes to purchase a flat outright they acquire a 99 year lease. Those members who cannot

afford to do this enter into an option and agreement to purchase, known as the 'Sundowner Package'. Under this the initial payment a member makes is made up of two elements.

The first is the deposit, which is used to reduce the size of the mortgage attributed to their flat. The second is an advance which is used to reduce the member's contribution to the repayments on the outstanding mortgage down to a proportion of a fair rent. (The larger the initial payment the lower the rent they have to pay.)

For example, with a flat costing £25,000 (1985 prices) and a mortgage rate of 12.75%, a member could pay the minimum deposit of £6,000 and their weekly rent would be £25.14. A member electing to make an initial payment of £15,000 would pay a weekly rent of £13.23.

At any point a member can buy the lease of their flat by paying off the outstanding mortgage loan. They remain a member of the co-ownership association but the only payments they make are to cover the provision of common services and repairs at cost.

Income from the rent is used to service the 'interest only' mortgage, pay the rates and insurance, and a non-profit service charge to the association for the maintenance of the fabric of the building, care of common parts, and provision of support services (which might include a resident warden or a 'good neighbour' alarm system). Those on supplementary benefit are eligible for the same sort of assistance as any owner occupier, including payment of the mortgage interest, rates and 'approved service charges'.

The rent is raised each year in line with inflation and any surplus used to repay the capital on the mortgage loan. The annual payments due on the interest-only mortgage do not include money for repayment of the capital sum. This is repaid by the housing association as money becomes available from surpluses raised on the rent, and deposits from people buying into the scheme.

Members enjoy the benefits and responsibilities of owner occupiers, coupled with suitable support services at a cost that can be tailored to meet their circumstances. The schemes rely on the expertise of the parent housing association, initially in assuring the lenders of the viability of the project, in managing it through all the development phases, and thereafter in providing management services to the co-ownership association.

The Sundowner package is designed for the particular circumstances of elderly people who are living in their own homes which are not appropriate to their needs, or who have some capital of their own. The parent association provides everything at a price intended to match their means. The principles behind the scheme potentially have a wider application wherever groups of householders can be identified with common needs associated with their housing.

The scheme has been worked out to maximize the benefits available. Tax relief is available on the whole of the co-owners' mortgage payments. Most of their rent would be paid by the DHSS if they were on supplementary benefit. Their savings can be put into the scheme to pay off the capital debt on their housing in a way that ensures these savings are not counted as capital that might disqualify claims for supplementary benefit.

Self-help co-ownership schemes

The Sundowner scheme is a rather complicated example of a co-ownership, reliant on the professional expertise of a housing association. But there are others that have been set up by people working to solve their own housing needs. These are also financed with a mortgage on the property as a whole, paid for out of rents paid by the members living in the property.

100% mortgages are only available on new build schemes. Co-ownership schemes generally depend on their members providing capital to bridge the gap between the amount a lender will advance against the security of the property and the costs of purchase and conversion. This is loaned to the co-ownership association in the form of loan stock (see below). It is the equivalent of the deposit a house owner normally expects to put down in buying their house.

Why form this type of co-ownership
Generally speaking it is easier to raise mortgages on long leases (99 years or more) on each separate unit than it is to raise one mortgage on the property as a whole. It is harder to manage the property when everyone must contribute to keeping up the payments on one mortgage. Complications arise when anyone leaves and wants to take out their share of the value of the property. These are dealt with below in considering how to finance co-ownerships (see page 89).

But there are a number of reasons why a group might decide to form this type of co-ownership:

• It may not be practical to divide the property into self-contained flats. It is sometimes possible to fit more people comfortably into a shared house than into the same property divided into flats.

• You may want extensive shared facilities, perhaps with a common dining room and catering kitchen, with facilities for no more than small meals to be cooked in individual units.

• You may plan to convert the property into self-contained units yourselves over a period of time, and need to finance it in this way for two or three years while the work is in progress. This allows for more flexible use of the property while the work is in progress.

- Another reason is that the co-ownership as a whole might be able to raise a mortgage where some members might be unable to do so in their own names. The lender will be concerned to see that the group as a whole can afford the repayments.

If there are not many people involved, it would be simpler to form a joint-ownership trust as described in chapter 4. There must be at least seven to form a co-ownership.

Financing a co-ownership through the rents

Co-ownerships financed through the rents are financed in the same way as housing co-operatives, with a mortgage on the property as a whole. Some lenders prefer co-ownerships to co-ops, believing that because the members have a financial stake in the property they will take greater care of it.

You are unlikely to raise all the money you need as a mortgage loan. House owners usually reckon to put up some of the money from their own savings or other sources. In a co-ownership the members put their 'deposit' in in the form of loan stock.

Loan stock

Drawing up a loan stock certificate is very simple. There is an example of one in Appendix C, and your solicitor or accountant should be able to help you with it.

You can set the terms and conditions to suit the particular circumstances of the loan, covering the amount of interest to be paid, and the terms of repayment. These can be whatever you require so long as they are unambiguous. You must keep good records in the form of a loan stock register with every loan stock certificate issued including its unique certificate number.

Instead of paying interest, some co-ops index-link their loan stock so that it increases in value in some relation to the change in property values. It might seem appropriate to link it to the House Price Index, but if it is index-linked to anything other than the Retail Price Index the increase may be taxable as a one-off interest payment when the loan is paid off, with the Inland Revenue effectively taking nearly a third of it.

If you want to maintain the real value of money loaned to a co-ownership or co-op, index linking to the Retail Price Index attracts less tax than paying the equivalent amount of money in interest. Any interest you pay on top of index-linking is taxable in the usual way. The co-op is required to send details to the Inland Revenue of any interest it pays. Payments made in repaying a loan index-linked to the Retail Prices Index do not have to be declared.

There are a few co-ownerships, mostly in large rural properties that cost very little per unit to purchase, that have used index-linked loans in this way to raise most of the capital they required to purchase the property. When someone joins, they have to put in their share of the value of the property in return for loan stock index-linked to the Retail Price Index. The size of the loan grows with inflation so that when they leave they take out a sum of money larger than they came in with. This money generally comes from the person who joins the co-ownership to replace them.

Money loaned under the terms of your occupancy agreement is not included when the DHSS assesses whether your savings take you over the limit for supplementary benefit, provided it is made clear to them that the loan is a condition of occupancy. In practice you need not declare savings that are invested in loan stock in your housing to the DHSS.

Raising a mortgage loan

Few branch managers will have experience of lending to a co-ownership, or to any form of housing co-operative. It may be better, particularly on a large scheme, to apply to the regional or head office of the building society concerned. The local branch office should be able to tell you whom to approach.

You will need to put together a package of information to introduce yourselves and provide answers to some of the questions that would concern a lender. This information should include:

- The legal status of your co-ownership society;
- A copy of your occupancy agreement and explanation of the way this confers ownership rights on the occupants;
- An explanation of how the co-ownership plans to raise the money paid to departing members and any implications this may have for remortgaging the property;
- A calculation of the rents, showing that they will be sufficient to meet loan repayments and other expenses;
- Any track record the association may have, especially in managing its financial affairs;
- Details of your members, their jobs and incomes;
- Details about sources of additional finance;
- Full details of any specific property on which you are seeking a mortgage, including details of any renovation work you will be undertaking;
- Where extensive renovation is being done, give details of bridging loans and where the finance for this is coming from;
- Information on your professional advisers, and recognition from other bodies such as the Housing Corporation or local authority.

These points are all discussed under their respective subheadings below.

The legal status of your co-ownership

You must be a 'fully mutual', 'equity sharing', housing co-operative. All these terms are explained earlier in this chapter and are defined in the glossary in Appendix D.

You should also have applied for approval under section 341 of the 1970 Income and Corporation Taxes Act. You get this from the Department of the Environment (or relevant Secretary of State for Scotland or Northern Ireland). It gives tax relief on the interest element of the mortgage payments on a loan of up to £30,000 per unit at 1987 values (or per tenancy of a shared housing scheme), and exempts the co-ownership from paying tax on any profit arising from sale of its property, or from rental income.

All the high-street building societies and banks operate the MIRAS scheme, under which they claim the tax relief subsidy on the mortgage interest for you, and charge you correspondingly reduced mortgage payments. Approval under section 341 means that you are eligible for MIRAS (see chapter 2, page 20).

It is very simple to apply for approval, by writing to the relevant Secretary of State enclosing copies of your rules and the co-ownership agreement or lease under which your members occupy the property. They will then ask all the relevant questions. Your solicitor or accountant should be able to advise you, or do it for you.

The lender will want proof of your registration with the Registrar of Friendly Societies − a photocopy of your registration certificate will do. The certificate will be attached to the back page of the copy of the rules that the Registrar returns to you when you are registered.

Include a copy of your rules, and, where applicable, proof of your registration with the Housing Corporation.

The Co-ownership agreement

The co-ownership agreement defines the right of each member to occupy the property, and might specify which rooms or which unit will be theirs. The agreement also says how their share of the rent is to be worked out, and might include details on their responsibility to co-operate with the other members in managing the property. In a co-ownership the agreement also specifies how a co-owner's share of the value of the property is to be worked out when they leave.

A hypothetical example might help to illustrate the possibilities. This one is based on the terms used by the trust described in chapter 4:

1. Each person's 'share' in the value of the property is defined in their agreements as a proportion of the total value.
2. Their share of the mortgage loan is also defined in their agreement. It is worked out as the net cost of providing their share of the property, less any 'deposit' they pay in the form of loan stock.
3. Their rent is made up of their 'share of the mortgage payments' (from 2 above), plus their 'share' (as defined in 1 above) of the management and maintenance costs as determined by a general meeting of the association.
4. Anyone wishing to leave must give six months' notice, during which time the property is valued by a valuer approved by the mortgagee (the lender). They can leave earlier if anyone can be found to replace them within that time.
5. When they leave they are entitled to their 'share' (from 1 above) of the valuation of the property, from which is deducted the outstanding loan on both their share of the mortgage (from 2 above) and their loan stock. They are also entitled to repayment of their loan stock (which is index-

linked to the Retail Price Index, but attracts no interest).

6. The person coming in to replace them takes over their 'share' of the property, and responsibility for their share of the mortgage. They must also pay a 'deposit' sufficient to cover the payment made to the departing member.

7. If nobody has been found to replace them after six months, and no other way has been found to repay them, the members all receive three months' notice of termination of their agreements, and the whole property is put on the market for sale by auction at the earliest possible date. The association is then wound up. Under these circumstances each member receives their share of the profits arising from the disposal of all the association's property after payment of all its debts.

In practice, under this sort of agreement, those remaining might choose to take over the share of the property vacated by someone who was leaving, rather than find someone to replace them. Or they might take over some part of it, so as to reduce the burden and make it more attractive for a newcomer, particularly if they were having difficulty finding someone suitable to take their place.

Once you have discussed these issues amongst yourselves and written what you want to do in plain English, you should ask your solicitor to incorporate your requirements into an occupancy agreement.

Raising the money for departing members
A particular problem that arises for co-ownerships is finding the money to buy out the person who is leaving.

If this money is coming from someone new coming in to replace them, how does the new person raise the money to 'buy in'? Without a saleable lease on their own self-contained unit the newcomer will be unable to raise their own mortgage in the conventional way in order to pay their share of the current market value of the property.

At the start you may have raised quite a large proportion of the purchase costs as a mortgage so that the original members only had to find a small proportion from their own resources. But those buying in later will have to find all the money paid to the person they replace. After a few years of high inflation this could amount to a very high proportion of the value of their part of the property.

This problem is similar to the one faced by trusts. The most satisfactory solution is to be able to remortgage the property every few years. The extra money is used to pay out people who are leaving.

Under the example agreement given above, the new mortgage would be in the name of the co-ownership. The existing members would remain responsible for the same size of mortgage loan as before. The newcomer would carry the burden of the extra mortgage, but they would not need to provide all the money paid for their predecessor's share of the increase in value as an extra deposit in cash.

Some building societies dislike co-ownerships because of this implied liability to remortgage the property whenever money is needed for someone leaving. As with trusts, it may be necessary to reassure them that your group will be fairly stable, and to arrange things so that it is unnecessary to remortgage more often than every two or three years. Inevitably with a larger group, people are likely to be coming and going more frequently than that.

You should also consider the implications of people buying in later having to pay more than the orginal group. After a few years there will be some people paying very much higher rents than others for living in the same house.

If you are living in self-contained flats you may be unaffected by how much it costs your neighbours to stay in theirs, but if you are living together in the same house these differences could cause problems. Those who have been there longest will not only know more about how the whole place runs, they will also seem to benefit most from it.

This may be the reason why there are not many co-ownerships operating in this way in shared housing. Most co-ownerships are based around relatively self-contained accommodation.

If you are planning to live together in a shared house, you should consider either forming a housing co-operative in which you effectively rent your housing, or find ways to temper some of the inequalities that would arise from the sort of co-ownership agreement given in our example.

You could, for example, consider increasing the 'shares' of the property ascribed to those who have been there longer, with a corresponding increase in the part of the mortgage they are responsible for. When someone 'buys in' they would then own a smaller proportion of the property. But they would also have to pay a smaller proportion of the mortgage, and provide less money as a deposit.

Under this approach, everyone's rent would have to go up to shoulder the burden of the extra mortgage payments, but the result would be that everyone's rent could be kept more or less the same.

This could be refined further, by planning rent rises each year so as to build up a reserve out of which loans could be made to someone buying in to replace a departing member. This would reduce the frequency of the necessity to remortgage the property.

It is quite possible, by a combination of measures such as these, to keep the cost of living in the co-ownership fairly even across the membership, without introducing any element of subsidy from one member to another. There is, of course, no magic here that would give you something for nothing. What you would be doing is increasing the share of the property owned by those who had been there the longest. One consequence is that it could prove very expensive to pay off someone who had been living in the property for several years.

The other way of evening out the costs is to pay less than 100% of the increase in value of the property to people who leave, and use the saving to reduce the cost to those moving in. The co-ownership agreement could exclude those who leave within their first two years from any share of the increase in value of the property. It could also pay out between 75% and 90% of the increase in value, rather than all of it.

Working out an agreement that can meet the aspirations of your individual members within the finance available from your lenders will take some careful thought and negotiation. You must consider the 'worst case' and limit your commitments to what can be done under those circumstances.

Types of mortgage

You might consider the various types of mortgage described in chapter 2. They would reduce the initial repayments, and hence hold down the weekly rents. But they would also reduce the amount of money you could take with you when you left.

With an index-linked mortgage the outstanding debt is increased each year in line with inflation. The debt could more or less keep pace with the rising value of the property, so there would be less build-up of 'equity' to be shared out when you leave, except from repayments on the loan itself.

Those in a co-ownership who are on supplementary benefit are entitled to assistance with the interest on their mortgage, but not with capital repayments. With an index-linked mortgage a larger proportion of the repayments are of capital.

An equity mortgage would reduce the weekly payments, but only part of the increase in value of the property belongs to the co-ownership, and hence would be shared out to someone leaving.

It is unlikely that a lender would agree to remortgage the property if you had one of these special types of mortgage, in order to help raise the money to pay out someone who was leaving. This is because the amount owed to the lender increases during most of the life of the mortgage. In fact you could look upon these forms of mortgage as effectively 'remortgaging' the property every year, because they have a similar effect: your payments go up each year, and the amount you owe also rises, for at least the first twenty years of a 35-year mortgage.

You would also find it very hard to obtain these special types of mortgage, since they involve extra risks which the lender will only undertake in certain circumstances.

Rents, budgets and cash flow
You need to be able to show that the rental income is sufficient to cover all outgoings in managing the property and servicing any loans. The income will need to cover:

- mortgage payments, and payments on other loans (including interest on loans from your own members)
- repairs and maintenance
- rates, and insurance
- administration, including audit fees
- a voids allowance to cover gaps between one member leaving and another joining.

Your co-ownership agreement may prevent someone leaving before they have been replaced, in which case you can leave out the voids allowance. Otherwise it is usually estimated as 4% of gross rental income.

Each year the Housing Corporation (see glossary) sets standard allowances for maintenance of property funded by Housing Association Grant. In the absence of any historic or other basis for estimating your long-term repair and cyclical maintenance costs, you might consider basing your figures on their allowance levels.

Budgeting enables a group of people to manage the finances of an organisation in a positive and constructive fashion. It is a way of putting down on paper what income is expected and where it is coming from, and matching this with estimates of different categories of expenses. The group as a whole (or its management committee) can then delegate responsibility to certain people to ensure that spending is held within the budget limits, or report back to them if changed circumstances make it necessary to modify the budget. In a similar way they can keep an eye on income.

A cash-flow chart takes the budgeted income and expenses and estimates the amount that will occur in each month of the year. From this you can work out how much cash you are likely to have at the end of each month, and make sure you will always have enough to pay your bills.

Once a housing co-operative or co-ownership is running it is a relatively simple matter to draw up budgets and cash flows, and calculate the rents required. Your accountant should be able to help you the first couple of times, after which you should be able to do it for yourselves.

Details of your members
Anyone lending you a mortgage loan will want to see that your rental income is sufficient to meet all reaso-

nably expected outgoings, and that it does not over strain the incomes of your members.

A bank or building society considering a mortgage loan will want a list of your members with their jobs and incomes, in order to assess whether they can afford the loan repayments. They may also want employers' references in order to check on your income and likely prospects. This is no different from the checks they make on an individual raising a mortgage loan.

There is no fixed formula by which they judge the size of mortgage loan that you could reasonably afford to repay. But as a rough guide, they may take 2½ to 3 times the income of the half of the group with the highest incomes, plus the gross income of the rest. They may also take account of the cost to you of servicing any other large loans on the property.

Recognition from other bodies
A co-ownership is a form of housing co-operative. Local Authorities and the Housing Corporation are able to provide assistance to you in a number of ways. Most of these are described in more detail in the chapter on housing co-operatives, since support is more likely to be given to a body providing rented accommodation, especially if it is helping those in greatest housing need.

The Housing Corporation can provide help to self-build schemes, particularly in finding bridging loans to finance them during the building work. They may also help you obtain land or buildings from a local authority on favourable terms, and help with training in the particular skills required.

You should discuss your plans with the Housing Corporation at an early stage. If you are planning to do a significant amount of renovation work, or build new housing, you should ask them for any information they have to help self-build societies.

The Housing Corporation will also be able to put you in touch with any secondary co-operatives or housing associations working with housing co-operatives in your area. These usually have their own architects and accountants as well as professional housing management and development staff, who can give advice and could play quite an active role in helping you find the right property and develop it, as well as in getting hold of grants and loans.

What about Housing Benefit?

As far as Housing Benefit regulations are concerned, you are in a co-ownership and treated as an owner if you are entitled under your occupancy or membership agreement to any payment determined by reference directly or indirectly to the value of the dwelling.

Members of a co-ownership are treated as owners rather than as tenants. You will not get any assistance with the rent on the grounds of low income. If you are unemployed or on supplementary benefit you should be eligible for help with your share of the interest charges on the mortgage, rates, and 'certain approved service charges', just like any other owner-occupiers.

It makes no difference whether the mortgage interest is paid through a rent or directly by you. In a 'leasehold co-ownership' you own the lease outright in the same way as anyone else buying a flat in a larger property, with your own mortgage and responsibility for rates. In other co-ownerships you pay for it all through your rent. In either event the assistance you get is the same.

For the first four months on supplementary benefit this assistance is reduced to cover only half the mortgage interest.

CHAPTER 7

Housing co-operatives

TENANTS OWN PROPERTY COLLECTIVELY
& MANAGE IT THROUGH A HOUSING CO-OP.

What is a housing co-operative?

The members of a housing co-op are tenants, each
with their own tenancy or occupancy agreement and
many of the same rights as other tenants. Although
they do not own the property individually, they own
it collectively and manage it through the housing co-
operative. Unlike the members of a co-ownership

BYHWOP—G

97

they do not have any personal stake in the value of the property.

The simplest way of setting up a housing co-op is to register it with 'model rules'. There are a number of organisations that have developed sets of rules for housing co-operatives, including the National Federation of Housing Associations (NFHA), and the Empty Property Unit at Shelter (EPU). The National Federation of Housing Co-operatives (NFHC) is working on a range of rules suitable for different sorts of co-op, and may well become the best source. They are in the process of registering the sample rules in Appendix B as model rules.

Having chosen a suitable set of rules, the members of the new housing co-op sign and register them with the 'Registrar of Friendly Societies' (see 'useful organisations and addresses' in Appendix D). Once registered, the co-operative can buy the property and grant tenancies to its members.

Types of housing co-operative

There are about 500 housing co-ops around the country. About 220 of these have been set up with public funding from local authorities or the Housing Corporation in much the same way as housing associations. These co-ops provide permanent accommodation for their members, under 'fair rents'. They are variously referred to as 'permanent housing co-ops', 'fair-rent co-ops' or 'HAG-funded co-ops'. This last refers to the 'Housing Association Grant' system of funding housing co-ops (see chapter 2, page 32). Publicly funded co-operatives of this sort are outside the scope of this book. To find out more about them contact the Housing Corporation, the NFHA, or the NFHC.

Other housing co-operatives occupy property that is due for demolition or redevelopment, through a 'licence agreement' under which the co-op as a whole agrees to vacate once the owner needs it back. Individual people occupy the property under a 'sub-licence agreement' with the co-op. Co-ops offering this sort of tenure are generally known as 'short-life co-ops'. There are a great many of them, particularly in London. Shelter's Empty Property Unit is the best source of advice if this is what you are considering. Once again these are outside the scope of this book. The bibliography gives details of other sources of information.

The housing co-operatives we are interested in are the privately financed housing co-operatives . There are about 50 of them, owning the property they live in, which was often bought with a mortgage loan from a bank or building society.

They have three important characteristics:

- They are 'fully mutual', which means that every member of the co-operative is a tenant or prospective tenant, and every tenant is a member. In other words the co-op is owned and controlled by the people living in its property.
- They are 'par value' which means the tenants have no stake in the value of the property. Literally 'par value' means they own the same amount, which is the £1 (or some such) share they bought on joining the co-op. When a member of the co-op leaves they do not receive a sum of money calculated to represent any part of the value of their share of the property. This distinguishes them from the co-ownerships described in the previous chapter.
- They are mortgage funded. They may receive improvement or repair grants, or any number of other grants. They may also borrow some money from their own members or friends in the form of loan stock (see page 103). But the difference between the money raised from these sources and the cost of buying the property is raised as a mort-

gage loan. This distinguishes them from 'publicly financed' co-ops, where the difference between the cost of buying and renovating the property and the amount of mortgage that could be repaid out of a 'fair rent' is paid off by a Housing Association Grant.

Why form a housing co-operative
The advantage of a housing co-operative is that it is easy for anyone to join or leave — there is no buying or selling involved. When you move in, you sign an occupancy agreement laying out your rights and responsibilities, which you surrender when you leave. Unless you have loaned money to the co-op, no money changes hands. As a result, renting is usually cheaper than with any of the other options.

If all you want is to share a house with some friends, and you imagine that once one or other of you leaves the whole arrangement will end, then a housing co-operative is not for you. Unless, that is, you have no interest in sharing the value of the property, and simply prefer to be tenants for other reasons. One of the big advantages of being in a housing co-operative is that you qualify for Housing Benefit from the moment you become unemployed or if you are on low income or Supplementary Benefit.

In many ways a housing co-operative is the ideal framework for rented housing. Because nobody profits from it, you get good value for money and have a say in how the co-op is managed. If there were plenty of co-ops providing good quality housing to suit every income bracket, we might have a real choice between buying our own home and renting.

In the meantime the choice of rented accommodation in many parts of the country is rather narrow. Those who can afford to buy their own place can pick and choose from a much wider range of possibilities. In addition they gain an asset that is likely to rise in value with inflation, increasing further the housing available within their means.

It is harder to raise a mortgage loan for a housing co-operative than for most of the other forms of joint ownership covered by this book, although a great deal of progress has been made in recent years and the prospects for mortgage-funded co-ops are looking brighter.

Secondary co-operatives

Secondary co-operatives are set up to help housing co-operatives develop and manage their property. Most of their experience will be with HAG-funded or short-life co-ops, although much of their experience would also be relevant to a mortgage-funded co-op.

The secondary co-ops are managed by the housing co-ops they provide services to. In this way the co-ops effectively pool their resources to employ professional skills in developing more co-operative housing, either building it from scratch or by reno-vating older property. Secondaries also employ accountants who can advise co-ops on their financial affairs, and housing management workers who can advise on the problems of managing rented property.

Housing associations sometimes provide a similar service for housing co-ops, particularly in areas where there are no secondaries. These associations are usually larger than secondaries. Their main pur-pose is the direct management of rented housing, rather than to help co-ops in managing their own property.

These organisations are sometimes referred to as 'development agents', or 'management agents', depending on the service the co-op is receiving. There is some debate within the co-op movement about which is best of two approaches to manage-ment.

The first approach is where the co-op does all its own housing management, supported by training in the necessary skills. Advocates of this approach point to the greater sensitivity as well as degree of control that this allows the co-op itself, as well as financial savings.

Under the second approach, the day-to-day tasks of housing management, such as collecting rent and chasing arrears, are carried out by management agents. In this case, the co-op sets the policy and negotiates an agreement under which it is professionally carried out. This is favoured by those who see the burden of voluntary effort as a disincentive to co-operation, and prefer management matters dealt with at arm's length by people who are not part of the co-op.

It is quite possible to employ management agents to do part of the work, while members of the co-op do the rest for themselves.

Most existing mortgage-funded co-ops are quite small and do all their own management. But some lenders are beginning to prefer co-ops that have the support of a secondary co-operative or some other managing agent, particularly if the co-operative is looking for an index-linked mortgage.

Financing a mortgage-funded co-op

The capital to finance a privately financed housing co-operative generally comes from some combination of grants, personal loans, and a mortgage.

It is not often possible to raise all the money to buy a house and do any renovation necessary in the form of a mortgage. This is because the lender will want the security of lending less than the full market value of the property. But there are a few circumstances in which it might be possible to raise all the money that way.

The most common circumstance is where a group of tenants join together to form a co-op to buy out their landlord. In this case they would expect to buy their houses as sitting tenants, which considerably reduces the market value of their housing (perhaps halving it). Since they themselves are the sitting tenants, they can obtain a mortgage based on a vacant possession value.

Where Improvement Grants or Housing Association Grant are available it may be possible to cover the cost of buying and renovating the housing you need with a combination of grants and a mortgage, particularly if you can obtain the property cheaply in the first place. These grants are explained in chapter 2.

In most cases, some of the capital comes from members of the housing co-operative. This is loaned to the co-op in the form of loan stock.

Loan stock

There is no difference in the way a co-op and a co-ownership issue loan stock, so that everything said about it in chapter 6 is relevant to a housing co-operative (see page 84).

Problems can arise if the co-op is dependent on large loans from one or two members of the group. It may not be easy to raise other loans out of which to repay these people when they leave. In an extreme case it may be necessary to sell the property in order to repay them. A balance has to be struck between the rights of the lender and the needs of the co-op as a whole. It is probably wise to replace private loans with institutional ones wherever possible. In the meantime it may be wise to allow plenty of notice before repayment becomes due, so as to give the co-ops some time to arrange an alternative source of finance.

Money that is loaned to the co-op as a condition of

occupancy would be discounted by the DHSS in assessing whether a person's savings put them over the savings limit for Supplementary Benefit. In practice the DHSS generally ignores all money loaned to the co-op by members.

Raising a mortgage loan

The rest of this chapter goes through the information you would present to a potential lender. In the process it looks at other sources of assistance to you in financing your housing, and explains how mortgage funding for a housing co-op works. You will need to understand a fair amount of jargon. If you cannot understand it from the text, look it up in the glossary in Appendix D.

Building societies can see the boom in home ownership tailing off as it reaches 70% of households. The societies must either diversify or see a slowing up in their rate of growth, and some are actively looking at ways to finance rented property. The fully mutual housing co-operative is an attractive option. The societies are mostly interested in larger schemes using low-start mortgages to produce rented accommodation at a cost that compares favourably with a market rent. But there is no reason why they should not also lend to smaller co-ops, and a number of them are actively doing so. Indeed some building societies have laid down policies on lending to co-ops and have circulated them to their branches. Others are at an earlier stage and refer all likely looking applications to their head office for individual consideration.

Housing law is very complex, and there is no reason why mortgage managers should have the experience fully to understand where your type of housing co-operative stands. You may have to apply to the regional manager of the building society, or direct to their head office. The local branch office will tell you whom to contact.

It is up to you to put together a convincing package that answers the kind of questions the lender will be concerned with. These include:

- the legal status of your housing co-op
- the nature of the tenancies created
- a calculation of rent and comparison with market rents
- any evidence of recognition by other bodies, e.g. local authority or Housing Corporation.
- details of your members, their jobs and incomes (particularly the first time they lend to you, they want to know the sort of people they are dealing with)
- your co-op's track record, especially in managing its financial affairs
- where the co-op has no track record, some evidence of the abilities of your members to manage the co-op effectively
- sources of any additional finance
- full details of any specific property on which you are seeking a mortgage, including details of repairs and alterations at the start of the scheme.

The following sections look at these matters in more detail.

The legal status of your housing co-operative

You will be a 'fully mutual', 'par value' housing co-operative. You will also have been approved under section 341 of the 1970 Income and Corporation Taxes Act by the Department of the Environment (or Secretary of State for Scotland), which gives you tax relief on the mortgage interest under the MIRAS scheme. The lender should be sent a copy of the letter conferring this approval.

These terms are explained earlier in this chapter, and are also defined in the glossary in Appendix D.

The lender will want evidence of your registration with the Registrar of Friendly Societies, and copies of your rules and occupancy agreement.

The nature of the tenancies created

If your tenants have security of tenure the lender could not get them out in order to sell the property should you fail to keep up the mortgage payments. Unless the lender can be assured of vacant possession if they need to sell following a breach of the mortgage agreement, they will assess the value of the property by its rental income. Since this is likely to be considerably less than a valuation based on vacant possession, they will reduce the amount they are prepared to lend accordingly.

Similar problems will arise under the new legislative proposals. What were secure tenancies look like becoming assured tenancies, under which tenants retain security.

There are a number of solutions:

Shared Tenancies. Housing co-ops in which the members live together in shared housing can avoid the problem altogether. Under their occupancy agreement they share essential facilities, including at least the kitchen or main living room – sharing just a bathroom is not enough. If you intend to share fully in this way, you will not create a secure tenancy. If you break the mortgage agreement the lender can easily obtain vacant possession of the house.

Most lenders now accept that, where there is going to be sharing of essential facilities, a suitable occupancy agreement (such as the one at the end of Appendix C) is sufficient to remove any problems over secure tenancies. In order to protect the lender's position, you could propose that the use of an occupancy agreement in this form, or some variation agreed with them, be made a condition of the mortgage agreement.

Registration with the Housing Corporation. Under the Housing Acts, tenants of a fully mutual housing co-operative registered with the Housing Corporation do not have security of tenure.

Although the Corporation is usually willing to register a co-op for this purpose, it is a long process and involves both the co-op and the Corporation in a lot of paperwork. Where a co-op is providing self-contained accommodation, registration with the Housing Corporation is nevertheless the simplest way of avoiding the creation of secure tenancies. The Corporation does not actively monitor such a co-op, and would only intervene in their affairs if persuaded to do so by one of the parties involved.

Token Co-ownership. Anyone entitled under their membership or occupancy agreement to ' ... a sum calculated by reference directly or indirectly to the value of the dwelling house' is defined as a 'co-ownership tenant' by the 1977 Rent Act. They are regarded as owners, so that their tenancy is not protected by the Rent Acts. Under pressure from lenders, some co-ops use a token form of co-ownership as a way of avoiding the problem of tenants' security of tenure. This is simply done by inserting a clause into the occupancy agreement under which occupants are entitled to some minute proportion of any increase in value of the property.

Some lenders regard this as the safest way of avoiding problems of security of tenure, though from the tenants' point of view it is a very poor arrangement: they lose all entitlement to Housing Benefit as well as the protection of the Rent Acts, without gaining the right to a payment when they leave that they could use as the deposit on buying their own home. They would have the same entitlement as home owners to assistance with their share of the interest payments on the mortgage, and with their rates. Generally speaking you should only accept this option if all other ways of avoiding security of tenure are closed to you.

Assured Tenancies   These were introduced in the 1980 Housing Act to enable landlords to develop new properties for letting at market rent. The idea was that the removal of rent control would result in an increase in the provision of rented housing, without disturbing the rights of tenants to a fair rent under their existing tenancies.

Under the government's new proposals, as they will apply to co-ops and housing associations, assured tenancies will replace previous forms of secure tenancy.

Assured tenancies are governed by the same rules as shops and other commercial lettings, under the 1954 Landlord and Tenant Act. The landlord can let vacant property for whatever it will fetch on the open market. Thereafter if the tenant objects to a rent rise they can apply to the court, in which case the court is required to set a 'market rent' which is then binding unless the landlord and tenant agree to another figure. This does little more than protect the tenant from victimization.

It is possible to evict under an assured tenancy by applying to the court on the grounds of persistent arrears, damage to the property, substantial breach of the tenancy agreement, or the offer of a comparable tenancy of a similar property in the area.

Under assured tenancies a co-op can charge any agreed level of rent. If the co-op and tenant cannot agree a rent, the court is empowered to interpret the terms of the tenancy in setting a rent. In the absence of a clear basis for reviewing rents, the court will set a market rent.

As a result, co-op tenants have security without rent control. A lender can value the co-op's property on the basis of rents chargeable under the tenancy agreement. This is an investment valuation, based on rental income. In practice some building societies will base their valuation on vacant possession, while others assess it as a function of rental income, having deducted management and maintenance costs.

Rental income

You should be able to show that the rental income is sufficient to cover all outgoings in managing the property. If you already manage other property under separate financing arrangements, you should break down the budget to show the viability of the new scheme within the budget as a whole.

The rental income must be sufficient to maintain an adequate cash flow, and to ensure the viability of the scheme. It will have to cover mortgage payments, payments on other loans (including interest on loans from your own members), repairs, rates, building insurance, administration – including the annual audit – and an allowance for voids and bad debts. Voids means those periods when rent is not paid between one tenant leaving and another moving in. The allowance is usually set at 4% of the total income from rents.

The lender will be concerned about how the resulting rent compares with rents charged in the neighbourhood. It should not be more than the local authority would be prepared to pay for someone who was unemployed or on Supplementary Benefit. In some cases this is somewhat more than a fair rent as assessed by the local Rent Officer.

At one time building societies wanted full details of each tenant, showing their income and financial status, in order to assess their ability to maintain the payments, in much the same way as they did for ordinary private house owners. This involved keeping them informed of every change in membership.

They also required at least the highest earners to sign an undertaking for 'joint and several liability', which meant that they could sue any of them for the amount owed by the co-op as a whole (despite the 'limited liability' of the co-op under which a member's liability for the debts of the co-op are limited to the value of their shareholding). As far as the lenders were concerned, this saved them having to take twenty people individually to court to get their money. Co-ops preferred that this liability be shared equally if it must be borne at all, and insisted on all their members signing the undertaking.

Building societies now vary on this. Some still require each member of a small co-op to sign a personal guarantee, although they are prepared to treat a larger group (of more than about 40 tenants) on their track record. Other lenders see this as unnecessary. Instead they are concerned that the cost of living in the property makes it an attractive proposition, and will be covered by Housing Benefit payments should the tenant's income drop, or they become unemployed.

When a co-op first applies for a mortgage, the lender may want details of your members' jobs and incomes because they want to know whom they are dealing with. If the co-op has a management agreement which provides it with a professional service from a secondary co-operative or some other housing management agent, the lender will not be so concerned about the individual members.

Co-ops try to persuade the building societies that so long as the rents are low in relation to what their members would have to pay elsewhere, and are below the ceiling that Housing Benefit would cover, their individual members' incomes are irrelevant. Rents in privately financed housing co-ops are, in any case, generally lower than the levels of mortgage payment most first-time buyers have to pay.

Recognition by other bodies

Local authorities
Some local authorities have a housing association officer to liaise with housing associations and co-ops within their area.

There are a number of ways a sympathetic local authority could help you, including:

- Making council property or land available for sale to you
- Providing improvement or Repair Grants (see chapter 2)
- Providing a mortgage loan
- Acting as guarantors to a loan from another body (this no longer counts as part of their capital spending programme), or making a revenue grant to make up the difference between a cost rent and a fair rent
- Supporting an application for registration with the Housing Corporation, or giving you a good reference in applying to another body for a loan. The Corporation invariably consults a local authority in considering an application for registration.

Local authorities will be interested in seeing an increase in the provision of good quality rented housing. They may be more prepared to support you if you are willing to absorb even a small number of people from their waiting lists as members of the co-op.

They will have to get consent from the relevant Secretary of State responsible for housing (the DoE in England and Wales) before they transfer property to you at below its valuation, guarantee a loan, or make a revenue subsidy (under section 58 of the 1985 Housing Associations Act). In practice this consent is generally withheld.

But there is nothing to stop them putting a condition on the sale of a property that it be used for rented accommodation for the next 50 years. This would reduce its valuation, and enable them to sell to you at a lower price without seeking specific consent from the relevant Secretary of State.

Martin Jelfs' book *Mortgage Finance for Housing Co-ops* gives more detail on the ways a local authority can help, together with tips on how to approach them (see bibliography).

The Housing Corporation
The Housing Corporation is keen to see an expansion of housing co-ops through the use of mortgage finance. Your first approach should either be through the nearest regional office, or through the co-ops officer at their headquarters in London (see 'useful organisation and addresses' on page 185. There is a number of things they can do.

They can act as guarantors for a loan from some other body, although they have only used this power in practice for overdraft guarantees to assist with development finance. They can also give a straight-forward mortgage, and have been known to do so.

They can provide Housing Association Grant (HAG) to a housing co-op that is registered with them. Most co-ops providing permanent housing have, to date, been financed with HAG. Briefly, the way it works is as follows.

The co-op receives HAG to make up the difference between the cost of developing a property and the level of loan that can be repaid with income from fair rents on it. As the fair rents are regularly reviewed they tend to rise, so that after a few years the co-op would begin to make surpluses. These are then 'clawed back' through a 'Grant Redemption Fund', leaving the co-op little control over its income.

Co-ops funded in this way are regarded as part of public-sector housing, and are beyond the scope of this book. You can find out more about the use of

HAG by contacting the Housing Corporation or reading 'Development – a Guide for Small Housing Associations' published by the National Federation of Housing Associations (see Bibliography).

The Housing Corporation has recently initiated a funding scheme in which it provides 30% of the costs of developing housing in the form of HAG, with the housing association raising the rest of the money through a building society mortgage and whatever other grants and assistance it can raise from other bodies. Any surplus is not then clawed back in the way described above. A co-op funded in this way is able to control its own affairs relatively independently once it is running.

At the time of writing, the proposals are very much at a pilot-scheme stage, and it is unlikely the grant would be available to a small co-op managing its own affairs without reference to professional development agents such as a secondary co-operative (see page 101). It seems that the grant will be available only to those with a proven track record, and experience in the use of mortgage finance. Initially at least, it will only be available on schemes that might otherwise have qualified for conventional HAG funding.

In all cases, the Housing Corporation will be concerned about the standard of accommodation provided, although there is no rigid application of a particular set of standards.

It is worth contacting the Housing Corporation early on so that they know who you are. They can sometimes help you to arrange a mortgage simply by confirming to the lending body that you are a bona fide housing co-op and that what you write about yourselves is correct. Building societies may be more impressed if they confirm, for example, that your tenants won't have security of tenure under a shared occupancy scheme.

Registration with the Housing Corporation is a

separate process from registering with the Registrar of Friendly Societies and is free. It takes at least three months.

Some lenders want to see the Housing Corporation, perhaps in conjunction with the National Federation of Housing Co-operatives (as the representative body for housing co-ops), setting and monitoring standards of management. This is both to ensure the property is adequately maintained and retains its value as security for the loan, and to avoid being caught up in any scandals of bad management, such as the messy business of having to evict tenants where the co-op had failed to maintain its mortgage payments. This is more likely to apply where the co-op has twenty or more members, since larger co-ops are more complex to manage.

If you have access to the professional expertise of a secondary co-op or other development or management agent, a potential lender may be more confident of the co-op's ability to manage its housing effectively over the lifetime of the mortgage. This would also reduce the co-op's dependence on key people with particular experience within the group.

Your track record

A co-op that has operated for a period, perhaps managing short life property, or housing funded in other ways, will be more attractive because it will be able to show a track record in managing its affairs. Give a brief history, the name of your auditor, and perhaps a reference from your bank manager.

Best of all is a record of regular payments. If you can show a good record of timely mortgage payments it will be easier for a mortgage manager to recognise you as a good risk. Once you have had your first mortgage for a couple of years they will be only too happy to lend you the money for more houses, especially if the value of your existing property has risen significantly in relation to your outstanding loans.

Newly formed co-ops will have to emphasise the qualities of individual members in assuring the lender of their ability to manage. Once again they will be more impressed if some of you have a good record of mortgage payments.

The property

Initial approaches should be made to lenders long before you identify any specific property. A loan application from a co-op will take much longer to process than one from an individual buyer, and your initial questions will concern their willingness to consider lending to a group such as yourselves.

You should also try to find out on what types of property they would be prepared to lend. They will be concerned that the property is readily resaleable at a price that allows plenty of safety margin, to ensure they can recoup their money. Valuation is a matter of judgement, and they might have their own ideas on what constitutes a safe investment. They don't usually like large rural mansions, for example, where the value of the property is low in relation to the cost of repairing or replacing any of it.

Getting good advice

It is not easy to assess the strengths and weaknesses of your own case, and this is where advice from people with some experience can be helpful. If you cannot find this locally, you could try asking the National Federation of Housing Co-operatives or one of the other national bodies listed in Appendix D.

If some of your members already own their own houses or have well paid jobs, you should be in a strong position to apply for a loan.

If your members have none of the trappings of middle-class respectability, you could press your local authority or the Housing Corporation for support on the strength of your housing need. The banks and building societies in Glasgow, for example, were keen to finance groups of tenants wanting to take over their housing on some of the most run-down estates, despite the fact that most of them were unemployed or single-parent families with plenty of social problems. But the tenants' groups were strongly supported by their city council and its housing department, who saw this as the most effective way to channel money into renovating the property and to encourage a return to a sense of community.

Different types of mortgage

Repayments on a conventional annuity mortgage stay the same while inflation reduces the real value of money. What may seem like a very expensive mortgage in the first years may seem relatively cheap as incomes rise with inflation.

After a few years a mortgage-funded co-op is likely to own an asset worth a great deal more than it owes on the mortgage loan. Because the co-op does not pay any of this increase in equity to its members, it goes on accumulating to nobody's benefit. Consequently there may be a temptation for the later members to try and wind up the co-op to get their hands on potentially large sums of money that have accumulated, though it was the earlier members who bore the greatest burden of mortgage payments.

The ideal mortgage for a housing co-operative would start with relatively cheap payments, which would rise at a little less than the rate of inflation. The co-op would trade short-term economy for future equity. A variety of different forms of mortgage designed to achieve this are described in chapter 2.

The initial payments on an index-linked mortgage cost about half as much as the payments on a normal mortgage. In subsequent years they rise in line with inflation. Since rent levels also tend to rise with inflation, the repayments on an index-linked mortgage match projected rental income much better than the repayments on a conventional annuity mortgage.

The outstanding loan, after allowing for any capital repaid during the year, is also increased annually by the rate of inflation so that its value is maintained in real terms. This is depicted diagramatically on page 35.

The main problem with index-linking the loan is that it leaves little scope for a co-op to raise more money on the property at a later date. The co-op might need to do this for a number of reasons, such as to carry out a major repair, or to adapt the housing to take account of changing standards, or to meet the needs of a different category of tenant. Since the repayments rise in line with inflation, there is no spare income from future rents to repay a further loan, except by raising the rents above the level of inflation.

Advocates of index-linking point out that on average incomes rise faster than inflation, and that the Housing Benefit system can protect those most vulnerable to rising costs. Although the outstanding debt rises for most of the period of the mortgage loan, it does so at a slower rate than inflation (see the diagram on page 35).

A co-op can do various things to take account of these problems. For example, the co-op could build a contribution to a reserve into the rents. Money from the reserve would only be spent on major repairs or renovation of the property. Another approach would be to use a mixture of index-linked and conventional mortgage loans, so that the repayments and the outstanding debt rose more slowly in relation to inflation.

Although index-linking provides a low-start mortgage, it is not low cost. The amount you pay in real terms is much higher than with a conventional annuity mortgage. This is partly due to tax relief being available only on the direct interest charge (currently around 4½%), and not on the money added to the loan each year due to inflation.

Deferred-interest loans can also reduce the initial cost of providing rented accommodation. The initial payments are usually between two thirds and three quarters of the amount you would expect to pay on a conventional mortgage.

Lenders may be unable to offer deferred-interest loans under the MIRAS scheme. Those on sufficient incomes could claim tax relief through their PAYE tax coding, or as a refund from the Inland Revenue. But those on low incomes or supplementary benefit would lose their entitlement altogether.

Building societies recognise that if they want to enter the field of rented housing, they must develop funding packages that more closely match mortgage payments to rental income. We can expect a number of new developments in the next few years. One of these could be an 'equity mortgage' under which the lender takes a share of the value of the property in exchange for a lower interest rate. The advantage is that tax relief is available on all the interest paid, making it good value for money.

As they move into the rented sector building societies will be anxious to ensure that their investment is safe. They will want to see a good standard of management of the rented housing, particularly where the outstanding loan rises for most of the period of the mortgage. Their initial bias is likely to be towards the larger, professionally managed schemes.

You may have to convince them of the viability of a small housing co-operative that you set up for yourselves. So far, none of those that have been funded by buildings societies has failed. If a co-op did fail to keep up its payments, it could do great damage to the prospects of other housing co-ops seeking to raise mortgage loans, so it is important for others as well as for yourselves that you fully appreciate what you are undertaking.

CHAPTER 8

Shared ownership

RENTED

BOUGHT

THE LEASEHOLDERS PAY RENT FOR THE PORTION THEY COULD NOT AFFORD TO BUY

What is shared ownership?

In a shared-ownership scheme the occupants have a stake in the value of their housing. They buy a lease on their own self-contained flat or house, usually from a housing association or a local authority, for a proportion of the value of the property. The leaseholder then pays a rent for the portion of the value that they could not afford to buy.

Someone wanting to live in a dwelling at 75% shared ownership, for instance, would buy 75% of the value of the property using a conventional mortgage from a building society. They would not normally have to pay a cash deposit. In addition they would pay a rent for the remaining 25% of the value of the dwelling, which would be based on 25% of what a fair rent for the dwelling would be. Under most shared-ownership leases the leaseholder can buy further chunks of the equity whenever they can afford to increase the size of their mortgage.

The idea was introduced in 1980 to help people who could not afford to buy a home outright, either because they did not have enough savings for the deposit on a house, or because they were unable to afford the full mortgage repayments.

Practically all existing schemes are set up and managed professionally by housing associations or local authorities. They cater for the needs of first-time buyers, with priority being given to housing association or local authority tenants.

The money to finance them comes from three sources:

- Sale of the shared-ownership leases. A 50% shared-ownership lease, for example, would be sold for 50% of the value of the dwelling as assessed by the district valuer.
- The mortgage loan raised by the local authority or housing association that holds the freehold, serviced out of the income on a fair rent charged on the portion of each dwelling that is rented. This is the landlord's mortgage, and should not be confused with the mortgage raised by the leaseholder to pay for the purchase of their shared-ownership lease.
- A grant from the local authority or Housing Cor-

poration to make up the difference between the cost of developing the property and the money raised from both the sale of the leases and the mortgage loan that can be repaid from the rents.

A few local authorities offer 'do-it-yourself' shared-ownership schemes to their own tenants, under which the tenant chooses the flat or house they want to buy. The local authority then buys it and leases it to them under a shared-ownership lease.

Although it is a relatively new idea, shared ownership has already been developed in a variety of ways. The principle, of a lease in which the leaseholder effectively owns a proportion of their home and rents the rest, can quite easily be defined legally.

Some building societies are considering operating shared-ownership schemes themselves, or through subsidiary companies. Under these the building society or its subsidiary would own the freehold, with the leaseholder buying as large a proportion of the value as they could afford using a conventional mortgage. As the leaseholder's income rises they can buy a larger proportion, so that eventually they can own the property outright. This is very similar to the equity mortgage described in chapter 2 (see page 28).

There is nothing to prevent a group of people jointly buying or developing housing to lease to themselves under shared-ownership leases, providing they can raise the finance. Some ideas for setting up a shared-ownership co-operative to do this are discussed towards the end of this chapter. But first, here is a more detailed explanation of the way in which conventional shared-ownership schemes run by housing associations work.

Conventional shared ownership

How does conventional shared ownership work?
A person wanting to join a shared-ownership scheme

buys a share of the property based on the district valuer's valuation, with the aid of a conventional annuity or endowment mortgage from a building society or bank. Their share may be as small as 25% or as much as 90% of the value of the property. There may be a minimum they must buy, but otherwise the proportion they buy is set according to the amount the purchaser can afford. This makes them the lease-holder of the dwelling.

The leaseholder pays a rent to the housing associa-tion for the remaining share of the dwelling. The Rent Officer assesses what a fair rent on the property would be if it were registerable, and the leaseholder pays a proportion of this rent according to the amount they are renting. For example, if they owned a 50% share of the dwelling through their lease, they would pay half the assessable rent, which would be adjusted to take account of their responsibilities for insurance, maintenance and repairs.

So the cost to the leaseholder is made up of mort-gage payments on the part they own, and rent pay-ments on the part they rent. The mortgage payments on a loan to purchase 50% of the property could be two or three times as much as the rent payments on the 50% they are renting. In expensive parts of Lon-don the difference is greater than on cheaper housing in the north of England.

They do not usually have to put down a cash depo-sit when they buy a shared-ownership lease. But they may have to pay legal fees, stamp duty and survey fees, although in some cases these too are covered by the mortgage loan.

The leaseholder normally has the right to buy a larger share of the property when they can afford the increase in their mortgage payments, in which case the rent payments would be reduced accordingly. They could buy it in stages, which are usually stepped in 25% blocks, so that they might start with

25% and buy a further 25% so that they own 50%. This is sometimes referred to as staircasing. Eventually the leaseholder might staircase up to own 100% of the equity, in which case, if they occupy a house, the freehold is automatically transferred to them, so that they become conventional home owners.

The shared-ownership lease
The leaseholder's rights and responsibilities are defined in a shared-ownership lease, based on a model lease published by the Housing Corporation.

If their lease is for a house, they will be responsible for all repairs and redecoration inside and out. Their rent will include a small service charge covering the costs of insuring the building, rent collection, and their share of the cost of cutting the grass and maintenance of any other common areas.

If they occupy a flat, the housing association will be responsible for all external maintenance and repairs, including exterior paintwork. The leaseholder would pay for this through their rent, which would include a service charge to cover their share of the costs of cleaning, lighting and maintaining all common parts, such as stairways and corridors. The leaseholder is responsible for all internal maintenance and redecoration.

They can sell their shared-ownership lease at any time. But unless they have staircased up to own it outright the housing association may have the right to nominate prospective purchasers and to restrict the sale price to the District Valuer's valuation at the time of sale, which may be less than they would get for it on the open market.

Tax relief and Housing Benefit
The leaseholders qualify for tax relief on the interest on their mortgage in the normal way, up to the usual £30,000 limit. This is usually deducted at source

under the MIRAS scheme.

If they become unemployed, they qualify for assistance in paying the interest on their mortgage in the same way as normal home owners. In addition they qualify for Housing Benefit to cover their rent payments.

Shared-ownership housing co-operatives

Self-help shared ownership
The most appropriate way for a group of people to set up their own shared-ownership scheme is as a fully mutual housing co-operative. The co-op takes over much of the role ascribed to the housing association in a conventional shared-ownership scheme. The individual members buy shared-ownership leases from the co-operative on their own self-contained flats or houses.

Without a grant the scheme would have to be fully self-financing. Rent levels on the rented portion would, in most cases, have to be higher than a comparable fair rent. If the housing co-operative could finance the rented portion of the scheme with an index-linked mortgage, or some other form of low-start mortgage (see chapter 2), it could still be cheaper than conventional home ownership. At the same time it could provide a means for a group of people to develop a sense of community in their own joint-ownership housing scheme.

Shared-ownership is relatively new, and has not yet been used by a self-help group. A number of co-operative shared-ownership schemes are in the process of raising the finance to buy and build their own housing. It appears that shared-ownership is taking over the role once played by co-ownership societies. In which case share ownership will become more familiar to lending institutions, and it will probably be easier to raise the money to acquire the housing for a shared-ownership co-op than for a co-ownership society. In the meantime the suggestions that follow are based on the principles developed for conventional shared ownership and the schemes currently being considered for co-operatives.

Financing a shared-ownership co-operative
The money to buy the site and build the houses, or to buy and renovate older property would come from a combination of three sources:

- Sale of the shared-ownership leases to members of the co-operative, who would each raise their own conventional mortgage from a bank or building society against the value of their lease. The members might pay some of the cost of their lease in cash.
- An index-linked mortgage, or some other form of low-start loan, taken out by the co-operative and repaid out of rents charged to the members under the terms of their shared-ownership leases.
- Any Improvement Grants or other grants the co-operative is able to raise (see chapter 2).

As with other schemes, a building society will not lend 100% or more of the valuation of the property. In order to make it financially viable, the co-op would have to find some way of ensuring that the property was worth more than the mortgage loans raised on it. This might be done by some combination of the following:

- Improvement Grants or other grants (see chapter 2);
- Purchase of the property at below full market value, either because the co-op includes existing tenants or owners of the property, or for some other reason;
- Cash deposits from members in addition to the price they pay for their shared-ownership leases. These would be used to reduce the size of the co-

operative's mortgage to the proportion of the valuation the lender was prepared to advance;

- Other loans in the form of loan stock (see chapter 6, page 84) from members or friends of the co-operative or any other source;
- Some other method of developing the property so that it was worth more on the open market than the co-operative paid to buy the site or buildings and do any building work necessary on it. For example, the members might do some of the work themselves. Or it may be possible to design and build the property for less than it is worth when completed.

At the time of writing, building societies are reluctant to lend on index-linked mortgages unless the co-op has a management agreement with an organisation capable of providing them with professional housing management. The societies may become more flexible as they gain experience both of shared-ownership and of low-start mortgages. Meanwhile it is up to your group to persuade them that you are capable of managing yourselves. Or the lender might be persuaded to accept an agreement under which the property is managed and maintained by the co-op members to standards which are monitored by the managing agents.

If the proportion of the equity that was sold to members under their leases was increased, the co-op would have to repay part of the index-linked loan. Building societies charge a premium for early repayment of an index-linked mortgage loan. For this reason, the leases should avoid giving the members the right to staircase, so that the members cannot buy a larger share of the value of their unit.

As in a co-ownership scheme, the co-op will have to decide the extent to which it has any say in selecting people who buy the lease and become members of the co-operative when a member sells up and leaves. The co-op could retain the right to nominate purchasers and set the price in relation to a valuation of the property. This would be specified in the lease.

Setting up a shared-ownership co-operative
The Housing Corporation or the NFHA may be able to advise you on where to obtain a suitable set of rules for a shared-ownership co-operative. The rules in Appendix B would also be suitable.

The co-operative's solicitors should be able to draw up a suitable lease, based on the Housing Corporation's published shared-ownership lease. This would be modified to remove staircasing, and to set a cost rent based on the cost of the co-operative's mortgage and other allowable expenses. If the co-op retains the right to nominate prospective purchasers, the lease should also specify how the selling price is to be agreed.

Some housing associations have set up similar shared-ownership schemes based on index-linked mortgage loans, and might be able to advise on a suitable form of lease. The equity section of the Housing Corporation may be able to suggest associations that have the relevant experience. A the time of writing, CDS Co-operative Housing Society in London, is setting up a similar shared-ownership scheme for a co-operative in the London docklands.

Having chosen a suitable set of rules and lease agreement, the co-operative would approach prospective lending institutions in much the same way as suggested for a co-ownership financed through the rents (see chapter 6, page 84).

Appendices
Appendix A

Sample trust deed

DECLARATION OF TRUST

PARTIES

1.   *Person A*
            (name and address)

2.   *Person B*
            (name and address)

3.   *Person C*
            (name and address)

            Person D
            (name and address)

            (further parties as required...)

hereafter referred to as ("the Parties")

Recitals

A.   By virtue of a Land Registry
            Transfer Conveyance dated the
            .... made between *(the seller)*
            and *persons A, B and C* and in

consideration of the payment by *person A, B & C* to the said *(the seller)* of the sum of £ . . . . the property known as . . . . (the "Property") registered with HM Land Registry with Title Number . . . . was transferred to *persons A, B & C* and subject to the rights and convenants more particularly referred to in the Registered Title but otherwise free from incumbrances.

B.

By a Mortgage (the "Mortgage") of even date the Parties charged the property with the payment to the . . . . Building Society as Mortgagees of the sum of £ . . . . with interest thereon and subject to the terms and conditions in the said Mortgage.

C.

It has been agreed between the Parties that they should hold the property jointly as Trustees for sale as Tenants in Common upon the terms of this Declaration of Trust for occupation by themselves and such others as they permit jointly as one household.

Provisions

Shares of Property

1. *Persons A, B, C & D (etc)* shall hold the Property in the shares mentioned below upon trust to sell the same with power to

postpone sale and shall hold the
net rents and profits until sale
and proceeds of sale on trust for
themselves as Tenants in
Common in the proportions (the
"Proportions") specified below:-

a) *Person A:* .... %
b) *Person B:* .... %
c) *Person C:* .... %
d) *Person D:* .... %
... *etc*

Shares of Mortgage 2. a) As between the Parties hereto
person A shall each be responsible
for the payment of ..... % (their
"Percentage") of the principle
sum of £ .... and all other
principle sums which may be
advance on the security of the
Mortgage and the interest
thereon and all other monies due
or hereafter becoming due under
the terms of the Mortgage (and
for the payment of their
Percentage of each and every
monthly instalment of principle
and interest due or hereafter
becoming due under the terms of
the Mortgage).

b) As between the Parties hereto
person B shall each be responsible
for the payment of ..... % (their
"Percentage") of the principle
sum of £ .... and all other
principle sums which may be
advanced on the security of the

Mortgage and the interest
thereon and all other monies due
or hereafter becoming due under
the terms of the Mortgage (and
for the payment of their
Percentage of each and every
monthly instalment of principle
and interest due or hereafter
becoming due under the terms of
the Mortgage).

c) As between the Parties hereto
person C shall each be responsible
for the payment of . . . . . % (their
"Percentage") of the principle
sum of £ . . . . and all other
principle sums which may be
advanced on the security of the
Mortgage and the interest
thereon and all other monies due
or hereafter becoming due under
the terms of the Mortgage (and
for the payment of their
Percentage of each and every
monthly instalment of principle
and interest due or hereafter
becoming due under the terms of
the Mortgage).

d) As between the Parties hereto
person D shall each be responsible
for the payment of . . . . . % (their
"Percentage") of the principle
sum of £ . . . . and all other
principle sums which may be
advanced on the security of the
Mortgage and the interest
thereon and all other monies due

or hereafter becoming due under the terms of the Mortgage (and for the payment of their Percentage of each and every monthly instalment of principle and interest due or hereafter becoming due under the terms of the Mortgage).

e) ... *etc* ...

Payment of Mortgage	3.	Each of the Parties hereto shall as between themselves and other Parties and without prejudice to the rights and remedies of the Mortgagee be liable to pay only their Percentage proportion of all principle sums and interest and other monies due under the Mortgage as set out in Clause 2 hereof and in the event of one of the Parties hereto paying more than such Percentage the other or others in respect of and to the extent of whose liability such payment is made shall upon demand repay the same to the Party making such payment.
Sale of Property	4.	In the event of the sale of the Property:-

1) Each Party to this Deed or their personal representatives (as the case may be) will pay from their Proportion of the proceeds of the sale their Percentage of the principle and other monies

payable under the Mortgage.

2) In the event of the share in the proceeds of sale of any of the Parties to this Deed being insufficient to cover their Percentage of the principle interest and other monies payable under the Mortgage their personal representatives (as the case may be) will pay the balance due to the said Building Society from their own monies and will keep each and all the other Parties to this Deed at all times indemnified from all claims costs demands expenses of whatever nature in respect of such balance.

3) Solicitors' and estate agents' fees and other costs incidental to the sale shall be disbursed from the total proceeds of sale before the parties take their shares in the Proportions and upon the terms and conditions contained in this Deed.

No further Mortgages

5. All the Parties to this Deed jointly and severally covenant with one another that they will not create or purport to create any charges mortgages liens or interests of whatever nature (other than the Mortgage) over or in respect of the Property or their respective shares in the Property or their respective proportions of the proceeds of sale of the Property.

Observe
restrictions

6. All the Parties to this Deed jointly
and severally covenant with one
another that they will at all times
observe and perform all
restrictions covenants conditions
and stipulations at any time
affecting the Property.

Repair

7. All the Parties to this Deed
severally covenant with one
another that they will at all times
keep the property in good and
clean repair and decorative
condition and will take such
individual action as may from
time to time be agreed to carry out
all repairs maintenance and
redecoration which the Parties to
the provisions of this Deed or the
Mortgage or under the rights and
covenants affecting the Property
and referred to in the Registered
Title.

Any parties may procure the
repair of the Property to the
following standard:-

1) The Property to be maintained
in good tenantable repair bearing
in mind the age and character of
the building.
2) That the exterior be decorated
every 4 years.
3) That the interior be decorated
every 5 years.
4) All fixtures and fittings shall be
kept in repair and renewed if
necessary.

For items of expenditure over £200 estimates shall be obtained and submitted to the other parties prior to the commencement of the work.

Costs   8.   Each Party to this Deed shall contribute their Proportion in respect of:-

a) The cost of the acquisition of any necessary fixtures for the Property.
b) The cost of any repairs decorations improvements or additions to the Property carried out with the joint agreement of the parties or under the provisions of this Deed or any works carried out pursuant to any of the covenants and provisions contained in the Mortgage or referred to in the Title of the Property or required by any statute order or regulation.
c) The cost of the insurance of the Property against fire and flood tempest storm earthquake impact from aircraft and articles falling therefrom and such other risks as the Parties shall agree for an amount to cover the full replacement cost including surveyors' and architects' fees.

Disputes   9.   If agreement cannot be reached as
on repairs   to whether particular works or acquisitions are necessary or on

any other matter connected with repair decoration improvement addition or replacement any Party may refer the dispute to a chartered surveyor appointed as in Clause 17.4 whose decision as an expert will be final and binding on all matters save those of law.

Division of rent or other income   10. Any income compensation rent profit or gain of any sort obtained directly from the Property shall be split in the Proportions. Except that any rent or other consideration obtained by the letting or licensing of any part of a Party's "Personal Area" shall be shared by splitting the nett proceeds two-thirds for the letting party and one-third to be divided between all the Parties if the letting increases the number of persons resident in the Property. The letting Party may retain all the nett rent or other consideration if there is no increase in the number of persons resident in the Property. "Personal Areas" shall be such areas as agreed from time to time between the parties.

Personal Areas

At this time the Personal Areas are as follows:-

1. *person A:* ....
2. *person B:* ....

3. *person C:* ....
4. *person D:* ....
5. ... *etc* ...

Accounts   11.1 The Parties to this Deed shall
procure the opening of joint bank
or building society accounts in the
joint names of all of the Parties to
this Deed and will make all
necessary arrangements which
may from time to time be agreed
by the Parties to this Deed for the
payment of all Mortgage
payments the cost of repairs
maintenance assessments and
outgoings payable in respect of
the Property (including all
general water and sewerage rates
all electricity gas water and
telephone charges) and any other
similar sums payable from time to
time in respect of the Property all
such payments being disbursed
from the said Bank Accounts.

11.2 The Parties to this Deed shall
make all necessary arrangements
amongst themselves for payment
into the said Bank Accounts of all
necessary monies to cover all
assessments and outgoings and
to ensure that the said accounts
do not become overdrawn.

11.3 All cheques standing orders and
direct debits on the said Bank
Accounts and all instructions to
the said bankers shall be signed

by any two of the Parties to this Deed.

Interest   12.   If a Party fails to pay his or her share of any amount due under this Deed or which under any rule of law or enactment is due to be paid in respect of the Property the other Parties may give good receipt to any tenant licencees or any other user for value of the Property who would otherwise pay the defaulting Party and if these amounts are not sufficient the debt to accrue interest at 4% over the National Westminster Bank base rate from time to time from a date seven days after the date of a written notice to the debtor invoking this clause until paid and such sums shall be a charge against that Party's share of the Property.

Tenancies   13.   None of the Parties to this Deed shall without the consent of all the Parties to this Deed grant or create or purport to grant or create any tenancy licence easement right or quasi-easement or similar matter in any way affecting the Property.

Use   14.   The Property only to be used as a private dwelling house for the joint occupation of the owners and such others if any as they shall agree shall live with them.

Pets   15.   No pets or other animals shall be
                      kept at the Property.

Termination   16.   Any party to this Deed may
of tenancies   require the termination of any
                      lease tenancy licence or easement
                      right or quasi-easement or similar
                      matter and the Parties to this
                      Deed shall take prompt steps to
                      secure the departure of any
                      person or body residing in the
                      house under such lease tenancy
                      or licence or that any easement
                      right or quasi-easement or similar
                      matter be brought to an end.

Sale   17.1 If any of the Parties to this Deed
                      shall desire to enforce the Trust
                      for sale to which the Property is
                      subject or to dispose of the whole
                      of his or her beneficial interest in
                      the Property that Party ("the
                      Selling Party") shall give written
                      notice (the "Sale Notice") to such
                      other Parties to this Deed as then
                      remain alive offering to sell the
                      whole of the Selling Party's
                      beneficial interest to the said
                      other Parties or any of them and
                      the other said Party or Parties
                      may within two months of the
                      receipt of such notice give written
                      notice ("the Option Notice") to
                      the Selling Party indicating a
                      desire to purchase the beneficial
                      interest.

Death of   17.2 If any of the Parties to this Deed
a Party   shall die whilst still in possession

of his or her beneficial interest in the Property and that interest shall not pass by will to all or any of the remaining Parties to this Deed then the Deceased's personal representatives (the "Selling Representatives") shall as soon as practicable after the death give written notice to such of the other Parties to this Deed as then remain alive offering to sell the whole of that beneficial interest to all or any of the Parties to this Deed and the other Party or Parties may within two months of the receipt of such notice serve an "Option Notice" on the Selling Representatives indicating a desire to purchase that beneficial interest at a price to be stated in the Option Notice. If no Option Notice is served Clause 17.8 shall apply.

Shares if no agreement 17.3 If more than one Option Notice is served within the time limit the Selling Party shall ascertain whether there is agreement as to the share each shall purchase. If there is not agreement the Selling Party shall sell each such share of his or her share as shall cause the remaining Parties to own equal or as nearly as possible equal shares in the Property.

Valuation 17.4 The Purchasing Party or Parties and the Selling Party shall attempt to reach agreement on the value of such beneficial interest on the open market at the time of the service of the last Option Notice such value to be taken as that proportion of the market value of the whole of the Property with vacant possession which corresponds with the Selling Party's Proportion and if such agreement has not been reached within two months next following the date of service of the Option Notice then an independent chartered surveyor shall be appointed to make a valuation binding on the Parties at the joint expense of the Selling Party and such other Parties as have served Option Notices such appointment to be made by agreement between the Parties or in default of such agreement by any Party from the firm of *(the local firm of surveyors)* or in default of them from *(another local firm of surveyors)* or their successors. Or in default of these appointed by the President for the time being of the Royal Institute of Chartered Surveyors.

17.5 From the time when such valuation has been agreed or made in the manner stated and communicated to the Parties (herein referred to as the "Valuation Date") the Selling

Party shall within ten days
thereof inform each other Party in
writing whether he or she is
prepared to proceed with a sale at
the price so agreed or determined
as aforesaid and if having so
agreed within 20 days of the
valuation date the Selling Party
receives notices indicating
willingness to buy at that price
the Purchasing Party or Parties
shall be bound from the date of
receipt of the notices to within
two months of the Valuation date
to pay the amount of the
valuation to the Selling Party and
he or she or they shall thereupon
make to the Purchasing Party or
Parties an assignment of that
beneficial interest free from all
incumbrances created by the
Selling Party or the deceased
owner and the Purchasing Party
or Parties shall not be entitled to
any abstract of title but shall
accept such title as the Selling
Party has save that the Selling
Party shall supply the Purchasing
Party or Parties with such other
evidence to perfect the titles as he
or she or they may be able to
provide and if the Selling Party is
a trustee of the legal estate in the
Property the assignment shall be
carried out in such a way as to
ensure that he or she does not
remain such trustee after its
completion. The current edition

of the National Conditions of Sale shall except where it is inconsistent with this Deed be deemed to govern the relations between the Parties once they become bound to sell and buy.

17.6 In the event that the Selling Party has not fully discharged his or her Percentage of the monies due under the Mortgage on the Property or any other monies due under this Deed such Selling Party shall discharge all principle interest and other monies payable by that Party under the Mortgage or this Deed from the proceeds of sale or if these are insufficient from their own monies.

Sale to third party

17.7 If for whatever reason the Parties do not become bound to purchase the whole of the Selling Party's share after the Selling Party has confirmed their willingness to sell at valuation then and only then the Selling Party may dispose of the beneficial interest to a third party who is approved in writing by the remaining Parties who shall be informed of the proposed sale price.

Enforcement of sale

17.8 If no purchaser has become bound or has unconditionally agreed to become bound to pay not less than the valuation price or any price agreed in writing between the Parties within seven months of the date of service of the Sale Notice then the Selling Party may enforce the Trust for sale (by sale of the Property with vacant possession at the next available auction organised by *(a firm of local property auctioneers)* to which the Property is subject and take . . . . or their nett share of the proceeds of sale after payment of all free in each case from the provisions of this Deed.

Resolution by drawing lots

18. If Parties each wish to purchase each other's share and cannot reach agreement, then by agreement they may select an independent person, agree in writing a valuation for each Proportion. Each Party wishing to purchase the whole Property should then select a different number from one to six, tell the independent person this number who should then roll a dice in all their presences and continue to do so until the number chosen by one of the Parties comes up. That Party shall then have the right to purchase the other Party's proportion at the valuation agreed and the Parties shall forthwith exchange contracts in the form of the current edition of the National Conditions of Sale for sale and purchase with vacant possession given by the Selling

Party a completion date not later
than two months from the roll of
the dice and the prescribed rate of
interest shall be 4% above the
base rate of the Midland Bank.

19.   Side or marginal headings shall
not effect the construction of this
Deed.

Copyright: Sinclair Taylor and Martin
9 Thorpe Close
Portobello Road
London W10 5XL

Permission will not normally be withheld for use of
clauses from this Deed by persons wishing to jointly-
own property in a trust.

Appendix B
RULES FOR A HOUSING CO-OP
(proposed NFHC Model Rules)

Name

1.   The name of the association shall be ....

.... Limited
[referred to in these Rules as the Co-operative].

Objects and powers

2.   The objects of the Co-operative shall be:
(a)   the provision, construction, conversion, improvement and management on the co-operative principle of dwellings exclusively for occupation by members of the Co-operative under the terms of an agreement [referred to in these Rules as the Agreement] granted to them by the Co-operative. The Agreement shall exclude any right for the members to dispose or transfer or assign the Agreement to any person or body other than the Co-operative or a member of the Co-operative and shall require the members to surrender or assign or transfer the Agreement to the Co-operative or a member of the Co-operative on their ceasing to be members.

(b)   the provision and improvement on the co-operative principle of land or buildings for purposes connected with the requirements of the members occupying the dwellings provided or managed by the Co-operative.

(c)   the support and development of bodies concerned with the promotion of co-operatives and the provision of co-operative housing.

3.   The Co-operative shall have power to do all things necessary or expedient for the fulfilment of its objects.

4.   The Co-operative shall not trade for profit.

Registered Office

5.   The registered office of the Co-operative shall be at:

....

Share Capital

6.   (a)   The share capital of the Co-operative shall consist of shares of the nominal value of ...... pound(s) each issued to members of the Co-operative upon admission to membership.

(b)   Shares shall be neither withdrawable nor transferable, shall carry no right to interest, dividend or bonus, and shall be forfeited and cancelled upon cessation of membership from whatever cause and the amount paid up thereon shall become the property of the Co-operative.

Membership

7.   (a)   The members of the Co-operative shall be those persons signing the application for registration of the Co-operative and those persons whose names are entered in the register of members [the Share Register].

(b)   Only tenants and prospective tenants of the Co-operative are eligible to become members.

(c)   Prospective tenants shall be those persons whose names are entered in a register of prospective tenants which shall be kept by the Co-operative.

(d)   A member shall hold only one share in the Co-operative.

8.   Application for membership shall be considered under the procedure laid down by the general meeting from time to time. If an application is approved, the Co-operative will issue the applicant with one share upon payment of the amount specified in Rule 6(a).

9.   (a)   A member shall cease to be a member if they:

(i) die, or
(ii) are expelled by a general meeting in accordance with Rule 9(b)(i), or
(iii) resign in writing to the Secretary or in person at a meeting, or
(iv) have their Agreement terminated, in which case they shall cease to be a member seven days after the Agreement

comes to an end, unless by that time they
have entered into a new Agreement with
the Co-operative, or

(v) assign, transfer or dispose of their
Agreement, or

(vi) cease to occupy the dwelling
provided by the Co-operative, or

(vii) are a prospective tenant and have
notified the Co-operative that they no
longer require accommodation provided
by the Co-operative, in which case their
name shall be removed from the register
of prospective tenants.

(b)　(i) A member may be expelled by a
resolution carried by the votes of . . . .
[being not less then one half] of the
members present in person and voting at
a general meeting of the Co-operative of
which notice has been duly given,
provided that a complaint, in writing, of
conduct detrimental to the interests of the
Co-operative has been sent to him or her
by order of the Co-operative not less than
one calender month before the meeting.
Such complaint shall contain particulars
of the conduct complained of and shall
call upon the member to answer the
complaint and attend the meeting. At the
meeting the members shall consider the
evidence in support of the complaint and
such evidence as the member may wish
to place before them. If on due notice the
member fails to attend the meeting
without due cause the meeting may
proceed in his or her absence.

(ii) No person who has been expelled
from membership shall be readmitted

except by a resolution carried by the votes
of at least the proportion required for
expulsion in Rule 9(b) of the members
present in person and voting at a general
meeting of which due notice has been
given.

Borrowing powers

10.   (a)   The Co-operative shall have power to
borrow money for the purpose of the Co-
operative in whatever manner it may
determine including the issue of loan stock,
provided that the amount for the time being
remaining undischarged of monies borrowed
shall not exceed £. . . . . . .

(b)   In the case of a loan from the Co-
operative's bankers, the Housing Corporation,
local authority, or any other public body, or on
a mortgage, the Co-operative may pay such
rate of interest from time to time as may be
negotiated by the Co-operative, but in the case
of loans other than mortgage loans from any
other source the Co-operative shall not pay
interest at a rate exceeding one percent per
annum above the . . . . Bank Plc base
lending rate for the time being or six and one
half percent per annum, whichever shall be
the higher

(c)   The Co-operative shall not receive money
on deposit.

(d)   The Co-operative may receive from any
persons donations towards the work of the
Co-operative .

(e)   The Co-operative shall have power to determine from time to time the terms and conditions upon which money is borrowed or loan stock is issued and to vary such terms and conditions subject to the provisions of Rules 10(a) and 10(b).

Management of the co-operative

11.   (a)   A general meeting shall be called by the Secretary giving each member of the Co-operative seven clear days notice of the date, time and place of the meeting, and of the issues upon which decisions are to be taken. The Secretary shall call a general meeting at the written request of not less than three members or one-tenth of the members of the Co-operative, whichever is the greater, who may proceed to call the meeting if the Secretary does not do so within fourteen days of receipt of the request.

(b)   No business shall be transacted at any general meeting unless one third of the Co-operative' s members or 25 of them, whichever is the less, are present throughout the meeting. If no quorum is present within half an hour of the time appointed for the meeting, the meeting shall stand adjourned to the same day in the next week at the same time and place, or such other time and place as shall be determined at the meeting and notified to the members; and if at the adjourned meeting a quorum is not present within half an hour of the time appointed for the meeting then the members present shall be a quorum.

(c) Every member present in person at a general meeting shall have one vote. Resolutions will be decided upon a majority vote of members present, except where otherwise specified in these Rules.

(d) The Co-operative may adopt Standing Orders from time to time governing the procedures of its meetings and laying down the manner in which its business shall be conducted within the Rules of the Co-operative.

(e) Until such time as a committee is elected under Rule 12:

(i) the management of the Co-operative shall be by regular general meetings (at least one in every three months) of all members present.

(ii) each general meeting shall elect a Chair who shall have a casting vote in the event of a tied vote which shall be cast in favour of the status quo, and whose function shall be to conduct the business of the meeting in an orderly manner.

(iii) general meeting of members present shall constitute the committee of management and have all the powers of the Committee under these Rules.

(iv) a general meeting shall have the power both to appoint and remove individuals, members or groups of members delegated to exercise certain powers on behalf of the Co-operative.

12.   (a)   A general meeting may decide by resolution to set up a Committee to manage the Co-operative. At all subsequent Annual General Meetings the Committee shall resign. A new Committee shall be elected, under the direction of the Chair, in accordance with procedures agreed by a general meeting.

(b)   The Committee shall, at their first meeting and subsequently after each Annual General Meeting, elect a Chair from their own number to hold office until the next Annual General Meeting. This person shall be the Chair of the Co-operative and may only be removed from office by a vote of two-thirds of the members of the Committee present at a meeting called for that purpose. In case of an equality of votes the Chair shall have a second casting vote which shall be cast in favour of the status quo. If at any general meeting or meeting of the Committee the Chair is absent or declines to act the members present shall elect one of their number to Chair the meeting.

(c)   The Committee shall consist of not less than seven or more than fifteen Committee members as determined by a general meeting, all of whom shall be members of the Co-operative. A general meeting shall determine the number of Committee members required to be present at a meeting while the Committee conducts its business.

(d)   The Committee may co-opt any persons to serve as Committee Members providing that there shall always be a majority of elected Committee Members on the Committee. Co-opted Committee Members may be removed by resolution of the Committee or of a general meeting.

(e)   Meetings of the Committee shall be called by the Secretary giving each Committee Member seven clear days notice of the date, time and place of the meeting, and the issues upon which decisions are to be taken. The Secretary shall also call a meeting at the request of two or more Committee Members who may proceed to call the meeting if the Secretary does not do so within seven days.

(f)   The Committee shall have power to do all things necessary in the management of the Co-operative except to determine those issues specifically designated as the responsibility of a general meeting under these rules.

(g)   The Committee may delegate any of its powers to sub-committees consisting of such committee members and other persons as the Committee shall think fit, provided that a majority of any sub-committee shall be members of the Co-operative. The powers delegated to a sub-committee shall be defined in written Terms of Reference.

(h)   A general meeting may remove any or all the members of the Committee by a resolution carried by two thirds of the members present and voting of which proper notice has been given to all members of the Co-operative. The general meeting shall then resolve by simple majority to manage the Co-operative by general meetings or proceed to elect a new Committee.

(i)   If a member of the Committee, or a close relative of theirs, has any interest in a matter under discussion by the Committee they shall disclose the nature of the interest to the Committee and may be required by any Committee member to absent themselves from the meeting while the matter is determined.

13.   The Annual General Meeting shall be held within three months of the close of the financial year of the Co-operative, the business of which will include:

(a)   the receipt of the accounts and balance sheet.

(b)   the appointment of an auditor.

(c)   the election of a Treasurer under the members' direction to be responsible for the proper management of the financial affairs of the Co-operative. The Treasurer shall hold office until the next Annual General Meeting unless removed from office and replaced by a general meeting.

(d)   the election of a Secretary under the members' direction who will have those functions enumerated in these Rules and such other functions as a general meeting may determine. The Secretary shall hold office until the next Annual General Meeting unless removed from office and replaced by a general meeting.

14.   The officers and committee members shall receive no remuneration for serving as officers and committee members.

15.   The Co-operative may invest any part of its funds in the manner mentioned in section 31 of the Act. The Co-operative may appoint any one or more of its members to vote on its behalf at the meeting of any other body corporate in which the Co-operative has invested any part of its funds.

Application of profits

16.   (a)   No portion of the income of the property of the Co-operative shall be transferred either directly or indirectly by way of dividend, bonus or otherwise by way of profit to members of the Co-operative except insofar as the Agreement may provide upon surrender to the Co-operative for payments to be made to the member.

(b)   The Co-operative may apply any profits towards carrying out the objects of the Co-operative.

(c)   Any profits not so applied shall be carried forward.

Audit and Annual Return

17.   (a)   The Co-operative shall in accordance with sections 4 and 8 of the Friendly and Industrial and Provident Societies Act 1968 appoint in each year one or more auditors to whom the accounts of the Co-operative for that year shall be submitted for audit as required by the said Act and shall have all such rights in relation to notice of and attendance and audience at general meetings, access to books and the supply of information, and otherwise as are

provided by the said Act. Every such auditor shall be appointed by the Co-operative at a general meeting, and in the case of any auditor so appointed who is a qualified auditor under section 7 of the said Act, the provisions of sections 5 and 6 thereof apply to his or her re-appointment and removal and to any resolution removing him or her or appointing another person in his or her place.

(b)   Every year not later than the date provided by the Act or where the return is made up to the date allowed by the Registrar not later than three months after such date, the Secretary shall send to the Registrar the annual return in the form prescribed by the Chief Registrar of Friendly Societies relating to its affairs for the period required by the Act to be included in the return together with:

(i)   a copy of the report of the auditor on the Co-operative's accounts for the period included in the return, and

(ii)   a copy of each balance sheet made during the period and of the report of the auditor on that balance sheet.

Minutes, Books, Seal

18.   (a)   Sufficient records shall be maintained and left at the Registered Office for the purposes of the Co-operative and to comply with the provisions of the Act

(b)   The Co-operative shall have a seal kept in the custody of the Secretary and used only by the authority of the Committee (or the general meeting until such time as a Committee is elected under rule 12). Sealing shall be attested by the signature of two members and that of the Secretary for the time being.

Amendment of rules

19.　(a)　Any Rule herein may be rescinded or amended or a new Rule made by a vote of three quarters of all the members of the Co-operative present at a general meeting where all members of the Co-operative have been given seven clear days notice of the change to be proposed at that meeting.

(b)　No amendment of these Rules is valid until registered.

Dissolution

20.　(a)　The Co-operative may be dissolved by the consent of three quarters of the members by their signatures to an instrument of dissolution provided for in the Treasury Regulations or by winding up in the manner provided for in the Act.

(b)　Upon a claim being made by the personal representatives of a deceased member or the trustee in bankruptcy of a bankrupt member to any property in the Co-operative belonging to the deceased or bankrupt member the Co-operative shall transfer or pay such property to which the personal representative or trustee in bankruptcy has become entitled as the personal representat ive or trustee in bankruptcy may direct.

(c)   A member may in accordance with the Act nominate any person or persons to whom any of his or her property in the Co-operative at the time of his or her death shall be transferred, but such nomination shall only be valid to the extent of the amount for the time being provided in the Act. On receiving satisfactory proof of death of a member who has made a nomination the committee shall, in accordance with the Act, either transfer or pay the full value of the property comprised in the nomination to the person entitled thereunder.

Interpretation

21.   In these rules "the Act" refers to the Industrial and Provident Societies Acts 1965 to 1978, or any Act or Acts amending or in substitution for them for the time being in force.

end of rules

Appendix C
Sample Occupancy Agreement

OCCUPANCY AGREEMENT

between

.... Co-operative Ltd (called the Co-op)

and

....

(called the Occupant) for the provision to the Occupant of accommodation at

....

THE CO-OP AGREES TO:

1. provide   (a) one bedroom for the use of the Occupant
    (b) kitchen, bathroom, living room and other communal facilities for shared use with other occupants.

2. improve and maintain the accommodation provided, to standards agreed by general meetings of the Co-op.

THE OCCUPANT AGREES TO:

1. maintain regular payment of the sum agreed by general meetings of the Co-op, being her or

his fair share, as determined by general meetings of the Co-op, of the amount needed for the purchase, improvement, maintenance and management of the accommodation provided;

2. co-operate with the other occupants to maintain a mutually acceptable living environment, as agreed by general meetings of the Co-op, having special regard to:
    (a) the general upkeep of the premises
    (b) the disturbance caused by noise
    (c) the use of shared facilities;

3. give one month's notice, either in person to a general meeting of the Co-op or in writing to the Secretary, of intention to resign from the Co-op and leave the accommodation;

4. surrender this Agreement to the Co-op on ceasing to be a member of the Co-op, for whatever reason, and terminate the occupancy forthwith, and not to dispose of, or transfer, or assign this Agreement to any person or body other than the Co-op, or sublet the accommodation to any other person or body.

IF THE TERMS OF THIS AGREEMENT ARE NOT UPHELD then the matter shall be referred to a general meeting of the Co-op to consider appropriate action.

THE PARTIES TO THIS AGREEMENT acknowledge that common principles of fairness and co-operation will be upheld in the interpretation and operation of this Agreement.

THE OCCUPANCY SHALL COMMENCE ON ...

Signed: ....(the Occupant)   Date ....

Signed: ....(for the Co-op)   Date ....

Loan stock certificate

ANY CO-OPERATIVE LIMITED
Anystreet, Yourtown, Someshire

Certificate Number . . . .

Date of Issue: the . . . . day of . . . .
. .in the year 19. . . . . . .

Any Co-operative Limited (hereinafter referred to as the Co-op) acknowledges receipt of the sum of
£. . . . . · . . . . . .

paid by

of

(hereinafter referred to as the Lender) to the Co-op on the following terms:

      1. Interest will be paid at the Midland Bank PLC's base lending rate, and will be due one year after issue of this certificate and at one year intervals thereafter.

      2. Repayment will be made within 30 days of receipt by the Secretary of Any Co-operative Limited of a written request for repayment.

In witness hereof   (Lender)
                             (Witness)
                                Date:

                     (Co-op Member)
                     (Co-op Member)
                           Date:

Examples of Alternative Terms:

1.   *No interest will be paid.*

2.   *On every anniversary of the date this certificate is issued the sum of money owed to the Lender shall be increased so as to inflate the sum owed by the rate of inflation determined by reference to the Retail Price Index.*

3.   *Repayment will be made within 30 days of the Lender ceasing to be a member of the Co-op.*

Appendix D
Glossary & other information

GLOSSARY OF TERMS

Annual Return   Each *housing association* or *co-op* registered with the *Registrar of Friendly Societies* is required by law to provide financial and other information by way of an annual return on a form provided by the Registrar. This is usually filled in with the help of accountants.

Assured Tenancy   A form of tenancy introduced in the 1980 Housing Act that is governed by the same rules as business and commercial tenancies (under the 1954 Landlord and Tenant Act). The dwelling must be self-contained, and either newly built or recently renovated. The landlord and each assured tenancy scheme must be approved by the *Secretary of State*. The tenancy is outside the normal provisions of the *Rent Acts*. The initial rent is as agreed between landlord and tenant. Following a rent review the courts will arbitrate to set a *market rent*.

Tenants have substantial *security of tenure* provided they can pay the rent. See page 58 for more detailed discussion.

Auditor

Chartered Accountant responsible for certifying that the accounts of an organisation are a correct and true representation of its financial affairs. *Corporate bodies* such as *housing co-ops* and *associations* and companies have to have their accounts audited each year.

Capital Gains Tax

A tax charged on profits arising out of the sale of property at a profit. Owner occupiers are exempt from this tax on their main place of residence. *Fully mutual housing co-operatives* are also exempted provided they are approved under section 341 of the 1970 Income and Corporation Taxes Act.

Company

A *corporate body* registered under the Companies Acts. Most companies are owned by their shareholders (some do not have shareholders, but have members who guarantee to pay the debts of the company up to a specified limit). Note that bodies registered under the Industrial & Provident Societies Acts are also sometimes loosely referred to as companies.

Co-ownership tenure

A form of tenure in which the tenant has a stake in the *equity*. A co-ownership tenancy is defined in section 86 of the 1977 Rent Act as one granted by a *co-operative housing association*, under which the tenant is entitled under the terms of their membership or occupancy agreement '....on ceasing to be a member and subject to any conditions stated in either agreement, to a sum calculated by reference directly or indirectly to the value of the dwelling house.' See chapter 6 for more detailed discussion.

Corporate Body

An organisation that is qualified to own property, make contracts, and act as a 'legal person' (corpus = Latin for body). Any legal reference to 'person' is assumed to apply to a corporate body as well as to an individual unless the context clearly excludes it. Most corporate bodies are registered under the Companies Acts or the Industrial and Provident Societies Acts (see *Registrar of Friendly Societies*). Their shareholders (or guarantors) have *limited liability*. A corporate body is taxed in its own right.

Cost Rent

A rent calculated as sufficient to pay the running costs of a tenanted dwelling, including the mortgage payments, insurance, voids allowance, and a reasonable sum for management and maintenance. In other words, it is the minimum rent that can cover a fair share of the costs of providing mortgage-funded rented accommodation, usually by a housing association or co-op. There is no recognition of the concept of a 'cost rent' under the *Rent Acts*.

Deferred-Interest Mortgage A *mortgage* on which repayments start low (in relation to anticipated levels of inflation) but are increased each year by a fixed percentage. This is achieved by deferring the payment of some of the interest in each of the early years and adding this deferred amount to the outstanding loan. Note that tax relief is only available on interest paid in any year calculated on the remaining balance of the original outstanding loan. See page 25 for discussion.

Development Agent An organisation providing professional help to a housing co-operative or a small housing association in the business of buying, building or renovating their housing.

DHSS Department of Health and Social Security.

DoE   See *Department of the Environment* under Useful Organisations above.

Equity   The inherent value of a property which can be realised when the property is sold. It is simply the market value of the property less the money owed on it.

Equity Mortgage   A mortgage under which the lender shares in the value of the property while lending money at a favourable interest rate on the property under a mortgage agreement. See page 28 for more detail.

Fair Rent   The rent fixed by the *rent officer* as being the maximum payable under a housing association tenancy or *regulated tenancy*. The rent is fixed for a period of two years and thereafter it may be re-registered every two years. In theory it is arrived at by looking at market rents in the area (ignoring local authority rents) and imagining what they would be if there were no shortage of housing. In practice the rent officers compare registered rents in relation to the type and quality of accommodation provided. See chapter 3 for more detailed explanation.

Fully Mutual   A fully mutual *housing co-operative* is one whose rules restrict membership to persons who are tenants or prospective tenants of the co-operative, and preclude the granting or assignment of tenancies to persons other than members. It was first defined in section 341 of the 1970 Income and Corporation Taxes Act for the purpose of giving tenants of fully mutuals the tax privileges normally available to owner occupiers.

Freehold   Land or property owned exclusively for an indefinite period. This contrasts with *leasehold*.

Ground Rent   The small rent (usually less than £150 a year) paid by the leaseholder to the freeholder under the terms of a typical long lease on the ownership of a property.

Housing Action Area   An area of housing designated by a local authority, in which living conditions are considered sub-standard. The local authority has extra powers in a HAA, including provision of higher levels of Improvement Grant. HAAs are part of a strategy for focusing resources on the improvement of an area of housing.

Housing Association Grant (HAG)

The main capital subsidy for *housing co-ops* and *housing associations* registered with the *Housing Corporation*. It is administered through the Housing Corporation or a local authority. The provision of *fair rent* housing by housing associations and co-ops is mostly funded under the HAG system, whereby the difference between the cost of providing the property and the *mortgage* loan that can be supported from fair rents on it is paid as a capital grant. HAG is also used to subsidise the provision of housing by housing associations in other ways, including provision of 30% of the development costs of certain mortgage-funded schemes.

Housing Association or Housing Society

This is defined in the Housing Associations Act 1985 as a society, body of trustees, or company set up for the purpose of (or whose powers include those of) providing, constructing, improving, or managing housing; or encouraging or facilitating the construction or improvement of housing; and which does not trade for profit. Most housing associations are registered with the *Registrar of Friendly Societies* under the Industrial and Provident Societies Acts 1965. Alternatively, they can be registered under the Companies Acts as companies limited by guarantee.

Housing Co-operative	A form of *housing association* providing housing for rent, in which management is under the control of the tenants. A co-operative housing association is defined by the 1985 Housing Associations Act as a fully mutual housing association. But non-fully mutual housing co-operatives also exist, in which there are some non-tenant members or non-member tenants. *Co-ownerships*, in which the tenants have a stake in the equity, may come within the legal definition of a housing co-operative, but are not generally regarded as such.
Housing Corporation	See under Useful Organisations and Addresses
Improvement Grant	A grant from the local authority for the purpose of improving rented or owner-occupied accommodation to an agreed standard. See page 30 for more detail.
Index-Linked Mortgage	A mortgage which starts with low repayments that are increased each year in relation to the rate of inflation (as measured by the *retail price index*). The loan

outstanding is also increased annually in line with inflation so that its purchasing power is fully protected. Typically the initial payments are around half the levels of the equivalent conventional mortgage.

Joint Tenants   If you own the freehold with others you will either be joint tenants or *tenants in common*. As joint tenants you own the property in shares, and if one dies their share passes automatically to the other owner(s). See also *tenants in common*.

Leasehold   Land or property which an owner has the right to occupy for a specified period, after which the property reverts to the *freeholder*. Leasehold is generally used to refer to long leases of 99 years or more. Those with shorter leases are generally referred to as *tenants*. Under the Leasehold Reform Act, some leaseholders have the right to buy the freehold to their property.

Leasehold Co-ownership   A *co-ownership* association in which the members own long leases on the dwellings they occupy, against which they individually raise mortgages to fund the purchase and renovation of the property.

Licence

An agreement to occupy a dwelling that does not confer a tenancy. Licences are used to provide short-life housing in properties that are awaiting demolition or renovation. Since the Street v Mountford case, it is likely that most licences are in fact tenancies, although if the property is to be redeveloped the tenancy would not be secure.

Limited Liability

The liability of the shareholders for the debts of most *corporate bodies* is limited (usually to the value of their shares, although it can be limited by guarantee to a certain nominal sum of money). This is designated by 'Ltd' or 'Plc' (for Public Limited Company) after the name of the body.

Listed Building

A building of special architectural or historic interest registered by the *Department of the Environment*. Special permission is required to alter or demolish the building. Grants are sometimes available for major repairs. Repairs and improvements to listed buildings are exempt from VAT.

Loan Stock

A loan to a *corporate body* that can be bought or sold. The corporate body should keep a register of loan stock issued with particulars of who owns it. They issue 'loan stock certificates' for the loan, giving terms of interest and repayment. Loan stock is paid out before trading debts in the event of liquidation. See page 84 for more detail, and Appendix C for a sample Loan Stock Certificate.

Market Rent
The level of rent that would be set in a free market in the absence of control by the *Rent Acts*. It will be higher in areas where there is a scarcity of rented accommodation.

MIRAS
Mortgage Interest Relief At Source is a scheme under which tax relief on the interest payments on a mortgage is deducted by the lender from the interest charged to the borrower. Under MIRAS you pay interest 'net of tax relief'. Tax relief is available to owner occupiers on the first £30,000 of mortgage on their main place of residence (1987 values). This limit accumulates for joint owners who are not married (there are proposals to limit the relief to one person per household in a new housing bill). It is also available to *fully mutual* housing co-operatives at the rate of £30,000 per tenancy.

Model Rules
The *Registrar of Friendly Societies* approves certain organisations as 'promoting bodies' with their own sets of rules suitable for use by any group. These rules are

called 'model rules', and if registered through the promoting body the fee for registration is reduced. The *NFHA, EPU* (and soon the *NFHC*) all promote sets of model rules suitable for housing co-operatives, as do some *secondary housing co-operatives*.

Mortgage

A loan secured on the value of a specific property. The mortgagee (lending body) usually holds the deeds until the mortgagor (borrower) has fully repaid the loan, and can force the sale of the property to recover their debt if it is not repaid. The mortgage is recorded on the record of the title deeds at the Land Registry. If the property is sold, the mortgagee is entitled to first payment from the proceeds of sale. The terms of a mortgage are governed by a mortgage agreement.

Par Value

A phrase used to described a *housing co-operative* in which the members have no stake in the equity. Literally it means 'equal value' and implies that all the members have the same interest in the property. Although HAG-funded co-ops are also 'par value', the term is sometimes erroneously used to refer to mortgage-funded co-ops. It should be used in contrast to the term *co-ownership*.

Protected Tenancy   A tenancy protected by the *Rent Acts,* which includes most private-sector tenancies in self-contained dwellings with non-resident landlords. Protected tenants have *security of tenure* and are entitled to have a *fair rent* registered. Tenancies granted by local authorities and housing associations are not 'protected tenancies', though they may be 'secure tenancies' under the Housing Acts (see *security of tenure*).

Rates   Local taxes comprising general rates and water and sewerage rates, levied on occupiers of property to pay for local services. Some landlords and landlord bodies collect the rates from their tenants on behalf of the local or water authorities.

Rateable Value   The value used by the local authority in calculating the *rates* it levies on the occupier of a property.

Redemption   Payment of the outstanding debt on a loan.

Rent Acts   Legislation controlling tenancies. The principle act is the Rent Act 1977, which defines *regulated* *tenancies* and housing association tenancies and instituted *fair rents*.

Registered Housing Association (or Co-op)

A *housing association* that is registered by the *Housing Corporation*. Note that it may also be 'registered' with the *'Registrar of Friendly Societies'*, but the term 'registered housing association' refers only to registration with the Corporation.

Registrar of Friendly Societies

The registrar is responsible for supervising Industrial and Provident Societies in a similar way to the Registrar of Companies.

Rent Officer

A statutory official whose duty is to establish *fair rents* at the request of landlords or tenants.

Retail Price Index

An index of retail prices that is published monthly by the government, and used as the basis for working out liabilities on index-linked loans. The use of any other index could result in tax liabilities from which loans linked to the Retail Price Index are exempted.

Secondary Housing Co-operative

A co-operative that is owned and managed by the housing co-operatives to which it provides services. These services usually include education in the business of running a housing co-operative, and the development of new or renovated housing, and may also include the provision of housing management and financial services.

Security of Tenure
A tenancy is described as 'secure' if the landlord's right to evict the tenant is controlled by the courts and limited to certain specific grounds, such as persistent rent arrears. Tenancies granted by housing associations (and co-ops) are defined as secure tenancies under the Housing Acts. Tenancies granted by other landlords are governed by the *Rent Acts*. Security under an *assured tenancy* is governed by the 1954 Landlord and Tenant Act.

Service Charge
A charge to the tenant by a housing association or other landlord for provision of services such as a communally run heating system, warden facilities, common rooms and cleaning, lighting and maintenance of common areas. Where the property is subject to the registration of a *fair rent* the service charge is part of the registered *fair rent*.

Shared Ownership
A combination of renting and purchase of a property, under which a person buys in relation to the cost of the dwelling as much

as they can afford in terms of mortgage payments, and rents the rest at the appropriate proportion of a *fair rent* from a housing association or local authority (see chapter 8).

Short-Life Housing Co-op

A co-op providing housing in property that is due for demolition or renovation, under *licence* from the developers (usually local authorities, but sometimes housing associations or other landlords).

Staircasing

The process by which the *leaseholder* under a *shared ownership* lease buys an increased share of the *equity*. This is usually bought in blocks or steps of between 10% and 25% of the value of the property.

Tenant

Someone who occupies a dwelling in exchange for rent.

Tenants in Common

If you own the *freehold* with others you will either be *joint tenants* or tenants in common. As tenants in common you own a specified proportion of the value of the property, and you can pass this share on to whoever you like when you die. See also *joint tenants*.

Trust

An organisation consisting of a body of trustees regulated by a trust deed, and for the benefit of specific 'beneficiaries'. Trusts are governed by the Trustee Acts. It is not a *corporate body*: its income and liabilities are regarded for tax and other legal purposes as belonging to the trustees (though not in their individual capacities). See chapter 4 for more discussion.

Voids

Periods during which a property is empty, for example the time between one tenant leaving and another occupying the property. 4% of rental income is commonly budgeted to cover loss of rental income through voids and bad debts.

Useful organisations and addresses

Coventry Churches Housing Association
A housing association which develops co-ownership associations specifically designed to meet the needs of the elderly, and a number of other forms of mortgage-funded co-operatives (see 'New Homes for Old' in the bibliography).

Highfield House, St Nicholas Street, Coventry CV1 4BR.

Department of the Environment
The *DoE* is the government ministry responsible for housing and environmental matters. In England and Wales the Secretary of State for the Environment at the DoE controls the *Housing Corporation* and has powers to control most of the housing activities of local authorities. In Scotland and Northern Ireland, these powers are vested in the Secretaries of State for Scotland and for Northern Ireland. In practice the DoE is invariably consulted on how these powers should be exercised.

2 Marsham Street, London SW1.

Empty Property Unit
Formerly the HEO, the *EPU* promotes the use of empty housing usually on a short life basis. It has

links to Shelter and the National Campaign for the
Homeless.

88 Old Street, London EC1V 9AX. (01 253 0202)

Housing Corporation

A statutory body responsible to the Secretary of State
for the Environment, who appoints the members of
its Board. It is the primary source of funding for
housing associations, and is responsible for
supervising and controlling housing associations
registered with it. It has regional offices throughout
the UK.

Head Office: 149 Tottenham Court Road, London
W1. (01 387 9466)

National Federation of Housing Associations

The *NFHA* is the central representative and
negotiating body for housing associations, providing
advice to associations and publishing the monthly
magazine *Voluntary Housing* and *Housing Association
Weekly*, as well as a number of useful books and
pamphlets on matters of concern to housing
associations and their tenants.

175 Gray's Inn Road, London WC1X 8UP. (01 278
6571)

National Federation of Housing Co-operatives

The *NFHC* is the representative body of housing co-
operatives, and received grant aid to fund its first full-
time workers in 1986. It aims to promote housing co-
operatives and represent their interests at every level.

88 Old Street, London EC1V 9AX. (01 608 2494)

Shelter
National campaign organisation for the homeless. It
shares offices with the Empty Property Unit and the
NFHC.

88 Old Street, London EC1V 9HU. (01 253 0202)

Bibliography

Collective Housing Handbook by Sarah Eno and
Dave Treanor, published by Laurieston Hall
Publications, Laurieston Hall, Castle Douglas,
Kirkcudbrightshire at £3.50 (£3.90 including post and
packaging). A practical manual on setting up and
running a collective household, including the legal
ways of collectively owning the property, ways of
raising the necessary finance, taxation and
accounting, and managing the collective way of life.

Mortgage Finance for Housing Co-operatives by
Martin Jelfs, published by the Empty Property Unit at
Shelter, £3.50. A guide to ways in which private-
sector money from banks and building societies can
be harnessed to provide rented housing for people on
modest incomes.

**Development – a Guide for Small Housing
Associations** published by the National Federation of
Housing Associations at £6.95. An explanation of
how to develop fair rent housing under the Housing
Association Grant system of funding.

Filling the Empties by Ross Fraser, published by
Shelter, £5.95. A manual for the management of
short-life housing.

New Homes for Old by Andrew Thomas, published
by Coventry Churches Housing Association, £7.50. A
guide to initiatives developed by Coventry Churches
to provide rented housing affordable by those in

greatest housing need, including the elderly, using mortgage finance from building societies.

A Handbook to the Industrial and Provident Societies Acts by Chappenden, published by the Co-operative Union.

Help 1: A basic guide to understanding jargon published by the National Federation of Housing Associations, £3. It explains the concepts and jargon found in the fields of both public and private housing.

Shared Ownership available free from the Housing Corporation, explains their shared ownership scheme under which people can buy as much as they can afford of a house or flat from a housing association, and rent the rest from them at fair rent levels.

Housing Legislation – a Guide to the Consolidated Acts published by the National Federation of Housing Associations.

Note that the National Federation of Housing Co-operatives maintains a list of books and pamphlets relevant to housing co-operatives, which can be obtained from them.

The National Federation of Housing Associations similarly keeps a list of publications pertinent to housing associations (including co-ops and co-ownerships).

Index